Shape Up or Ship Out:

A Message to All Political Parties

Shape Up or Ship Out:

A Message to All Political Parties

Maurice James Blair

Shape Up or Ship Out: A Message to All Political Parties

ISBN: 978-1-963470-12-3 (hardcover)

ISBN: 978-1-963470-26-0 (paperback)

Blair, Maurice James

Both the publisher Synapsid Revelations Press and the author M.J.B. have done their utmost to bear true and useful witness via the composition and publication of this. Consult if thou wilt with a sentient being or twenty-five or sixty-four or more if thou believeth it to fitteth thy situation.

This work is primarily intended as a semi-open book-length letter to whomever the author and/or the publisher may choose to arrange to receive at least one complimentary copy. The author can facilitate some such events by purchasing copies through online retailers as gifts to recipients. In contrast, the author can facilitate other such events through other means. Meanwhile, the publisher and the author are affording the general public the opportunity to purchase copies, though at the time of going to print the author neither expects to hold his breath nor to lose any sleep over waiting for anything other than modest sales to materialize. It is largely a courtesy to those affected that the publisher and the author are opening the door to members of the public voluntarily setting out of their own recognizance to purchase and explore it. Anyone who cares at all about whether any given political party lives or dies within a span of some number of years or centuries is affected by the message, whether any more than a handful of sentient beings ever bothers to read it or not.

Publication Date: January 9, 2025. Second Printing of Hardcover & First Printing of Paperback Inner text: After an initial transmission to the aggregation database when some time zones were in latter portions of January 9 (whereas others were in January 10), the publisher chose for the first printing of the hardcover to be approved with some typos, &c. noticed & a few unnoticed and to go to first print anyway. (See p. 79 for an explanation of part of why.) Paperback processing encountered an issue that delayed arrival to market. During that delay, the author and the publisher chose on January 13, 2025 to reduce typos; revision to be phased in: For first printing of the paperback to include cleaner copy, and for the hardcover's cleaner-copy second printing to wait until after paperback availability for sale. This is the 13 January 2025 edited version.

Synapsid Revelations Press
9619 Meadowcroft Drive
Houston, TX, U.S.A.

---

1 2 3 4 5 6 7 8 9 10 11 12 13 14 15 16 17 18 19 20 21 22 23 24 25 26 27 28

29 30 31 32 33 34 35 36 37 38 39 40 41 42 43

44 45 46 47 48 49 50 51 52 53 54 55 56 57 58 59 60 61

---

1. Political Science   2. Memoir   3. Social Psychology   I. Title

---

Premise

To: Each Existent Political Party Consisting of Beings

Cc: Anyone Else Who May Ever Read This

From: The Author of This Book

Subject: Shape Up or Ship Out

Date: January 5, 2025

For sentient beings to become enlightened—to whatever degree that may involve salvation, conscience, justice, equality, equity, meritocracy, liberty, and anything else of extraordinary worth to beings and their abilities to help others—is essential to their long-term well-being.

However, any specific political party, pair of political parties, trio of political parties, or other combination of political parties is in some sense expendable in the long run in the quest by sentient beings to achieve salvation, conscience, justice, equality, equity, meritocracy, liberty, enlightenment, and/or whatever else would be among the greatest and noblest of possibilities, because political parties that repeatedly fail to honor and respect major swathes of the populations of sentient beings tend to reap what they sow and can veer toward becoming replaced by better political parties. Think about how many political parties have bitten the dust over the millennia. Your party or parties could eventually become next to bite the dust and go extinct.

This is both the clear and coherent opening statement of this book and the clear and coherent closing statement of this book. From entrance to exit. From alpha to omega. From Om to Ah.

Introduction

The main set of pages of this work involves facts, screenshots, portions of screenshots, descriptions, transcripts, redacted screenshots, arguments, claims, counterclaims, and more descriptions.

Glean from these pages and their adjacencies what you will, and, if and when appropriate, consider possibly changing your mind(s) about what truth(s), facts, ideas, and implications you can arrive upon. *Although much of this constitutes a memoir spanning multiple decades, it is arguable that it more primarily serves as testimony about vulnerabilities of movements and tendencies for political parties to emerge, band together, rise, plateau, oscillate, fall, disband, and go extinct.*

An opening salvo: Think about the idea that no matter what anyone's demographics are and no matter what anyone else's demographics are, each and every individual, each group, and each and every organization tends to face consequences for thoughts, choices, attitudes, communications, and actions. Systematically dehumanizing anyone of any set of demographics, even in the name of fear that fuels an overprotection of any other set of demographics, can have deadly consequences in the long run. The alternative? Systematically humanizing each and every human may require difficult processes, including a willingness to let go of overprotecting anyone, yet it can heal communities.

Whether anyone is female, male, of a given ancestry, of a different given ancestry, of a given religion, of a different given religion, of a given economic status, of a different economic status, of a given social status, of a different social status, of a given party, of a different given party, of no party, or of any other category, if you harbor any bias against that anyone, then you are on track to cause both yourself and others much trouble, hardship, and tragedy. Consider now the contrasting way. Whether anyone is female, male, of a given ancestry, of a different given ancestry, of a given religion, of a different given religion, of a given economic status, of a different economic status, of a given social status, of a different social status, of a given party, of a different given party, of no party, or of any other category, if you choose to exhibit an unbiased way of showing genuine, due respect to that anyone, then you are on track to cause both yourself and others much mutual benefit and prosperity.

It could be helpful for a reader to study at least one of the previous publications from Synapsid Revelations Press prior to, concurrently with, and/or subsequently to studying this publication.

However, the publisher believes that there is still plenty of value that someone interested in the births, lives, and deaths of political parties and ideological movements might find by exploring this in the absence of studying any of this publisher's earlier books. Several of the books that Synapsid Revelations Press Corporation published before publishing *Shape Up or Ship Out* (2025) are:

- *I Am, Annotated Ninety-Fifth Anniversary Facsimile Edition* (2023) by F.C. Constable, with annotations by D.A. Blair and M.A.T. Blair / limited distribution as a free print book and freely accessible as a flipbook at https://mixam.com/share/654727341d4a1a0d3ac3f21d
- *Vajracchedika Sutra: Incisive Wisdom Beyond Normal Boundaries* (2023) by Unknown, with dueling translations by F. Max Müller and William Gemmell, including annotations by F. Max Müller and a transitional preface by Dwight Goddard / limited distribution as a free print book and freely accessible online at https://mixam.com/share/6525f88d9a328b561aad0144
- *Alternative Beginnings and Endings of All Things: Science, Religion, Politics, and Cards, Hypervolume II* (2024) and *The Dimetrodons, the Dorians, and the Modern World, Synapsid Critical Edition* (2024), both by Maurice James Blair / available for sale
- *Regarding Views and Regime Changes* (2025) by Yeshe Tsogyal, with annotations by Sir John Woodroffe and Synapsid Revelations Press, including use of Lao-Tzu, Unknown/Anonymous, and Synapsid Revelations Press quotes, edited by Synapsid Revelations Press; including main item translation by Sir John Woodroffe and Kazi Dawa-samdup; some supplemental quotes embedded in annotations translated by James Legge and F. Max Müller / available for sale

An Approximate Transcript of Portions of the Phone Call Between Johnny Courtland Ross II and Maurice James Blair on July 13, 2024 in the Wake of News Reports on That Day of an Attempted Assassination in Pennsylvania

Ross: What do you think would have happened if the attempted assassin had actually killed President Trump?

Blair: I think it would have probably guaranteed a Republican victory in November for the presidency.

Ross: Why do you say that?

Blair: Well, there are many Democrats and some Republicans who have long felt a deep personal animosity toward President Trump, and much of that would have no longer been a factor.

Ross: Interesting that you think that way, but I'm not so sure.

Blair: That having been said, there's something else kind of extraordinary about the sheer toughness that Trump showed in response to the attack.

There's a psychological proof level that President Trump is not actually all about himself, despite how you and many other left-leaning people claim it over and over again.

If he was all about himself, then he would have failed in a way perhaps resembling a specific scene from the movie *Dead Zone*—a great movie which starred Christopher Walken, by the way—but President Trump came through with flying colors.

He showed courage with how he cares more about the country than whether he lives or dies. Now, his critics can still allege him to be misguided, thinking inaccurately, or what-have-you, but if they keep claiming him to be in it all for himself, then that will seem clearly, obviously disingenuous to people who tune into how he showed courage in the face of an attempt on his life. Courage and grace under fire.

This could also relate to the *Knight Rider* episode "Trust Doesn't Rust."

An Approximate Transcript of Portions of the Phone Call Between Maurice James Blair and Johnny Courtland Ross II on or about July 21, 2024

Blair: Have you seen or heard the big news?

Ross: If you're asking about Biden dropping out of the presidential race, yes.

Blair: What do you think about this?

Ross: I am not happy about this. The Democratic Party has just shot itself in the foot. I don't think there's any way for the Democrat ticket for president to win this upcoming election, as its party leadership made the wrong choice.

Blair: Why do you automatically conclude that way? It's a long-ways-to-go before the election. Although I am leaning very much toward voting for Trump, it seems to me that there's still much uncertainty about how the next few months might unfold in terms of how much support the Republicans muster versus how much support the Democrats muster.
  What gives?

Ross: Look at Kamala Harris and her past.
  There's no way they're going to be able to get anywhere near electing her!
  I'm so disappointed in the Democratic Party leadership!

<u>An Approximate Transcript of A Portion of the November 4, 2024 Ted Cruz Rally in Cypress, TX, From a Q&A Session a While Prior to Cruz's Arrival at That Event</u>

<u>Texas Lieutenant Governor Dan Patrick</u> (indicating who should ask the next question, points toward Maurice James Blair, who was among the many present who were raising their hands in pursuit of asking Qs): Over there.

<u>Maurice James Blair</u> (inspired by a then-recent CBS News segment on the subject; curious about how much the TX Lt. Gov.'s statement might differ from how CBS News had presented several sides and facets of it): Would you please share comments on strength of foreign policy?

<u>Lt. Gov. Dan Patrick</u>: Could you repeat that?

<u>M. James Blair</u> (speaking louder): Would you please share comments on strength of foreign policy?

<u>Lt. Gov. Patrick</u>: I still couldn't quite hear that. Could you ask that again?

<u>A Female Acquaintance Standing to M.J.B.'s left as viewed from the audience & right as viewed from the stage / A Woman Who Appeared likely in her 20s or 30s</u> (shouting very loudly): WOULD YOU PLEASE SHARE ANY COMMENTS ON STRENGTH OF FOREIGN POLICY?

<u>Lt. Gov. Dan Patrick</u>: We have none.
   (He then provided a pregnant pause before resuming.)

<u>Lieutenant Governor Dan Patrick</u> (continuing his answer): Many people are wondering who's running the white house. It sure isn't Joe Biden.
   Who could it be?
   I think it could be President Obama actually running things from behind the scenes. When he became president he had a radical agenda. After no longer being eligible to run again after serving two terms, he sought another way to influence things. Only now, Biden and Harris have been able to go even more radical with policies than what Obama could do while he was president.
   Our nation's foreign policy has fallen apart. Other countries don't respect us right now, because they can tell that the Biden Administration is weak in dealing with our enemies. Just look at what's happened between Russia and the Ukraine, and look at how Hamas attacked Israel. Things have gotten so dangerous. We may even be on the brink of having World War Three.
   However, there's reason to hope.
   I believe we're going to witness a huge red wave tomorrow.

<u>An Approximate Transcript of Excerpts from the March 26, 2010 Health and Wellness Speech Presentations at West Chester University</u>

<u>ACEER President Roger Mustalish:</u> I'd like to thank our sponsors. ...
(Much later, he transitioned things into presenting a video.) Here's a video of several West Chester University programs. ...

(Quite a while later at the event, after the video and after additional speakers, ONJ spoke.)

<u>Olivia Newton-John:</u> Visiting West Chester University and the ACEER Foundation is very comfortable to me. Visiting them feels very much like visiting the university in Australia where my father served as a professor when I was a child. ...

(Much later: This next portion is possibly a hybrid of splicing together several separate portions of her keynote speech and/or an approximation of one portion of her speech, likely with resequencing of some of the semblances of sentences.)

<u>Olivia Newton-John:</u> It was in 1992. We were in waters near San Juan, and not having any whales visible there was *very* unusual. *Then I got the call that my father had passed away.* Not long after that, I received a call to go see my doctor.

When I found out I had cancer I went through several stages of grief. First, I reacted with laughter, then there was denial, then great fear. Eventually, I came to accept it.

The doctors had at first given a test to say that I didn't have cancer, yet my body kept telling me that something was wrong. Upon my insistence, they redid testing for what might be wrong, and it led to finding the cancer. This shows something very important: You have to listen to your body's messages. Sometimes it can be crucial to listen to your body when it tells you that something is wrong. I did that, and here I am all these years later.

Instead of liking to say that I am a cancer survivor, I prefer to say that after having survived the cancer, now I am a thriver! ...

(Much later, there arrived a question-and-answer session. Although her husband, "Amazon" John Easterling, helped her at times in addressing the inquiries, Olivia addressed most of the audience's questions without having him chime in. Here is a sample approximation.)

<u>A Person From the General Public:</u> What habits help to keep you healthy?

<u>Olivia Newton-John:</u> I exercise regularly, watch my diet, take wonderful herbs from my husband's company, and honor my role in maintaining a great marriage with Amazon John. Also, I've never been a smoker. {Instantly, portions of the audience burst into laughter upon hearing her characterize herself as having never been a smoker. It seemed that many people found incongruity between that statement and how a famous scene in *Grease* (1978) featured her smoking briefly.} {Note: Evidently, the extreme rarity of when she had smoked up to the time of that 2010 speech was such that, for the sake of simplicity, in some major sense she had given what might be considered a 98% truth. E.g., consider, "Olivia Newton-John was never 'really a smoker' up to then; she was among those who had virtually never smoked."}

[6]

A.T.A.S.C.W.B.:

A Transcript of A Semblance of A Conversation From About 2022 With a Bartender Who Pronounced His Name "David Bosa"

Patron M. James Blair: Did you do something for a while before you became a bartender?

Bartender Bosa: Yes. I was a professional auto racer for a while.

Blair: Really? That's interesting. Did you ever make it into the really big time?

Bosa: Mid-level racing.

Blair: Wow, so that was something like reaching Double-A baseball, wasn't it?

Bosa: Something like that.

Blair: There's something I've rarely asked anyone about, and, of the few asked, no one yet has had much of a clue how to answer it, but maybe you might be the first to give me a good answer to it.

Bosa: And what might that be?

Blair: After watching much Indy 500 coverage live from 1987 to the early 1990s, sometime in the early 1990s I noticed the Formula One driver Nigel Mansell make his Indy 500 debut. During some years leading up to that race I'd watched Formula One sometimes and cheered for Alain Prost, sometimes noticing Mansell as one of the most capable rivals to Prost and the other elite F1 drivers. Curious about what Mansell could accomplish at Indy, I soon found it astonishing when he consistently passed other drivers by going around outside of them on corners, adjusting the phases of where to accelerate and decelerate, and timing it just right repeatedly. I had not witnessed other drivers at the Indy 500 doing that method much at all, yet he was doing that over and over again. It was quite remarkable!
   What I wonder about this is why hardly any other drivers were doing that maneuver?

Bosa: Because they don't want to die! That maneuver was well-known long before Mansell's 1992 debut at the Indy 500, but it is an extremely high-risk maneuver.
   All it takes is a small mistake and—Bam!—you hit the wall hard and you're dead!
   However, there was at least one other driver who used that maneuver many times at the Indy 500: The great Jackie Stewart used it repeatedly and successfully decades before Nigel Mansell suddenly brought it back as a go-to method.
   Quite dangerous, but if someone dares try and succeeds at doing it well, then it can be very effective!

Table of Contents

Chapter 1: To Serve as Preludes and/or Trailers

Part I: Chronologically-sequenced transcripts of portions of several email messages, some of which also appear within screenshots many pages later, others of which appear only one in this work; plus commentaries:

A1. A Message Sent on August 3, 2011 at 11:01 A.M. CDT

From: (U.S. Citizen of the General Public) Maurice J. Blair

To: (U.S. FBI Agent) Marcus Padow

Subject: greetings, fellow Duke Alumnus

Marcus,

This is Jim Blair AKA Maurice AKA Hoser. Geoff Williams was kind enough to let me know how to reach you. Congratulations on finding a special career role!

If you don't mind my asking, did you get a chance to see *Transformers: Dark of the Moon*?

I missed the previous Transformers movies, though I watched some of the TV series when I was a kid, then I decided to watch this year's film installment. I really enjoyed it, especially since it seems to do for the space programs and geopolitics of 1961 to 2011 what Homer did for some of the warfare and political history involving Ancient Greece.

BTW, I don't know anything about D.B. Cooper other than publicly available information; however, imagining things related to his story in a style similar to some episodes of *The Twilight Zone* led to my development of a 2005 short story I wrote in April of that year and entered into the 74th annual version of a writing contest. I didn't officially win any awards from the contest, btw, lol ;-)

If you have any topics you'd like to discuss with me by e-mail or telephone, just let me know.

It's great to be back in contact with you after all these years!

YITB,

Jim Blair

A2. January 7, 2025 Commentary on the 2011 Message Transcribed to A1

The source message did not include italics, yet in the transcription I italicized portions that are more standard that way.

B1. Part One of A Message Sent on August 19, 2011 at 4:51 P.M. CDT
From: Maurice J. Blair
To: Ethan Ellenberg Literary Agency
Subject: SUBMISSION: Maurice James Blair
Ethan Ellenberg Literary Agency:

The past literary activities I have engaged in are unorthodox enough that some publishers would probably prefer to steer 20,001 miles clear of publishing my works anytime in the near future... However, there are probably at least a few publishers who would be very interested in the nonfiction project I am proposing here.

Proposed Title:

An 89-Dimension Approach to Creation, Preservation, Destruction, and Trade

Outline:
I. An Introduction
II. Overview of the Superstructure
III. The 56 Dimensions of the Minor Arcana
IV. Treating The Great Ultimate as a Transition Between the Minor Arcana and the Major Arcana
V. The 24 Dimensions of the Major Arcana
VI. Transitions from the Major Arcana to the Directional Energizers
VII. The 9 Directional Energizers
VIII. Foundations of the Unfathomable
IX. Exploring Some Sample Arrangements
X. Conclusions and Catalysts for Additional Research & Development

Sample from possible first chapter material:

On July 12th, 2011 I reflected on what artificial limitations someone might fall prey to if overvaluing my article "Perhaps the Dawning of a New Tarot Deck." Upon this reflection, in the spirit of exploring possible tonics, I chose to design something quite different. This resulted in an eighty-nine card system, which one could just as easily call an eighty-nine-dimension system, and I could sense right away that the powers encountered were of an extraordinary level of danger and opportunity. I resolved at first to keep my notes on this hidden, possibly to remain unknown to the public until some time after my death. However, on August 18th to 19th, 2011, I had a change of heart and considered sharing the pattern with others... carefully and selectively.

B2. Part Two of A Message Sent on August 19, 2011 at 4:51 P.M. CDT

Sample from possible second chapter material:

The Minor Arcana here includes four suits: Creators, Preservers, Destroyers, and Traders. Each suit has fourteen cards. These fifty six are...

The Ace of Creators, The Two of Creators, The Three of Creators, The Four of Creators, The Five of Creators, The Six of Creators, The Seven of Creators, The Eight of Creators, The Nine of Creators, The Ten of Creators, The Servant of Creators, The Manager of Creators, The Master of Creators, and The World-Beater of Creators,

The Ace of Preservers, The Two through Ten of Preservers, The Servant of Preservers, The Manager of Preservers, The Master of Preservers, and the World-Beater of Preservers,

The Ace of Destroyers, The Two through Ten of Destroyers, The Servant of Destroyers, The Manager of Destroyers, The Master of Destroyers, and the World-Beater of Destroyers,

The Ace of Traders, The Two through Ten of Traders, The Servant of Traders, The Manager of Traders, The Master of Traders, and the World-Beater of Traders.

The Major Arcana, arranged as pairs includes:

I. UNITY
XXI. THE GREAT ULTIMATE

II. DUALITY
0. NONDUALITY &/OR PLURALITY

III. METHODOLOGY
XVIII. UNKNOWN

IV. That of All Techniques and No Techniques
XIX. EXECUTION

V. RELIGION
XX. Moment of Truth

VI. PASSION
XVII. EXCAVATION

VII. PURSUIT
XVI. LAW

VIII. SUPER SYMMETRY
XV. SUPER CHAOS

IX. (a nonalphanumeric series of the three symbols The Swastika of Ganesha, The Swastika of Kali, and The Star of David)
XIV. (a nonalphanumeric series of the three symbols The Wheel of Dharma, The Celtic Cross, and The Star of Lakshmi)

[11]

XI. Popular Self-Help

XII. Ecclesiastes

(non-ASCII numeral of "Infinity Alpha"). Tetragram Models

(non-ASCII numeral of "Infinity Omega"). Voidness Models

Next, there are The Nine Directional Energizers.

Author Bio:

From sometime 2001 to June 2005 Maurice James Blair researched and developed some bizarre things involving the convergence of science, religion, psychology, economics, and spirituality. From June 2005 through August 2011 he continued to pursue a bold striving toward encountering things both substantial and supersubstantial. One of the highlights is the article "Perhaps the Dawning of a New Tarot Deck," published online by Aeclectic Tarot in June 2010. Another highlight is the present work.

Sincerely,

Maurice J. Blair

B3. Commentary on the 2011 Message Whose Copy Here Spans B1 and B2:

Although Ethan Ellenberg Literary Agency evidently refrained from directly responding to me regarding that book proposal, the main ideas involved with that proposal became major portions of the basis for *An Encyclopedic Survival Guide for Navigating Normal and Paranormal Experiences* (2023, a collective work for which I served as the main editor, distributed as a free online flipbook and as an intended-for-free-distribution paperback) and *The Science, Religion, Politics, and Cards Trilogy*.

  On another note, the only significantly noteworthy adjustment to the text in the transcription process was that I deleted the space between "some" and "time" in the phrase, "From some time 2001 to June 2005…" as displayed in the source message to render it above as the phrase, "From sometime 2001 to June 2005…"

C1. A Copy of One Paragraph from a Message Sent at 5:41 A.M. CST on December 23, 2024:

From: Maurice J. Blair (also known as Jim Blair)
To: Yin-Hsuan Chiu (also known as Sherry Chiu)
Subject: Fwd: Re: Universal Family Watch

Here is a reminder that although I am sometimes involved to some degree with the organization sometimes referred to as Nature-Loving Wonderland and at other times as Providence Maitreya or Maitreya Great Tao, of which you became a clergy member approximately in your early twenties, I am also involved with several other religious organizations and consider the competing guidelines, beliefs, and practices with a sense that the full reality may be beyond what any one of them can come anywhere close to fully expressing.

C2. A Comment on C1: Redacted Screenshots of This and Surrounding Context Appear Many Pages Later

<u>D1. A Redacted Copy of a 23 DEC 2024 at 6:15 A.M. CST Message From Maurice J. Blair to</u>
<u>Yin-Hsuan Chiu ("Sherry"), and featuring on the cc line inclusion of Liza Darnton, Alex Tse,</u>
<u>Ry Pickard, Tad Schmaltz, Dan Nolan, and Ming Blair</u>

Sherry,

Although, if you and my mother wind up with different versions of what you had said to her, if anything, in relationship with what she had characterized you as having said, I might not ever know for sure in this worldly life how much of the accuracy was with whom, whatever happens next should prove at least somewhat enlightening.

Please take a look at the portion of the forwarded email that has her advising me to conduct myself with filial piety taken to the extreme, alleging you to have corroborated with advocacy for that sort of thing for people in general and/or for it to specially apply to your case as of then. After taking a look at that, please see whether you deem it best to exercise your right to remain silent or to exercise your right to go ahead and write something to me--either as part of hitting "reply all," composing, and sending, or by another means of communication-- about your memory and reactions regarding it.

By the way, and this goes not only to you but also to the six cc line people, for clarification, in the forwarded message my statement involving my cousin Alex became typed before I added my mother to the list of cc line recipients in that prior communique. I intended originally only two to go on that cc line, then I changed my mind and added a third person to that line. Subsequently, I did not find and edit the line to correct that detail.

Although I recognize that you might be disappointed to find that Providence Maitreya Buddha Missionary Institute did not receive any reference in the forwarded draft of a last will and testament, the way that things have unfolded such that this present message is happening does involve acknowledgment of the Nature Loving Wonderland / Providence Maitreya religious organization having been one of the many religious organizations to have had a meaningful and helpful effect on my life, especially my ability to help other sentient beings.

Thanks for your role in proving helpful. I look forward to either your chiming in with a response or remaining silent. Either way, have a great day!

On another note, as your father Sam seemed perhaps on the verge of knocking on heaven's door when he and I last met approximately half a year ago, I shall mention wishing your family the best regarding his situation, whether he is still currently among those remaining in this worldly life or he is among the dearly departed. Also, best wishes to others in your family!

Again, Season's Greetings!

Jim

From: Maurice Blair
Date: Sun, Dec 22, 2024 at 8:17 PM
Subject: Fwd: A 28 AUG 2024 DRAFT LAST WILL & TESTAMENT, BEFORE ADJUSTMENTS
To: Liza Darnton; Dan Nolan; Ry Pickard
Cc: Tad Schmaltz; Alex Tse; Ming Blair

Liza, Dan, and Ry,

The aftermath of sending this message will possibly help with several determinations: 1) which services, if any, I might in the future hire Kirkus to do; 2) which services, if any, I might in the future hire other providers of review and/or editing services to do; 3) whether I someday return to the traditional model of creating manuscripts with which to send to agents in hopes of reaching mass market publication, rather than the straight-to-micropublishing method which I have done prodigiously in the past 27 months; 4) whether any and/or all of you might choose to take tangible steps toward swaying what I might decide in terms of determinations 1, 2, and 3.

It is surprising how much difficulty some people have with understanding my family sometimes. Here is an attempt to clarify such as to foster the improvement of lives in general:

*   *   *   *   *

After getting partway into Fall Semester 1994, early during my freshman year at Duke, inspired in part by the {starring David Carradine (1936-2009) as the protagonist} *Kung Fu* and *Kung Fu: The Legend Continues* TV series, in part by other popular cultural items, and, in very large part by the sometimes-mind-boggling and often-intriguing readings from the "Introduction to Philosophy" class that Dr. Schmaltz (who is among the cc line recipients of this message), a huge shift happened.

Specifically, it was similar to how some scenes from *Black Widow* (2021) involved variations of how mammals can sometimes deactivate visceral, strong affection--either in general or in specific relation to someone or something--and it was similar to how many religious ascetics have done similar ways of controlling some ranges of activating, deactivating, and reactivating that.

I had reached a way of using the mind to deconstruct the patterns of normal reality such that I could almost any time at-will turn on, turn off, or turn to some intermediate level affection for nearly anyone. It was crude early on, it sometimes went away entirely, there were rollercoasters of changes, and, in the long run, that ability became consistently capable and much more advanced.

In contrast with that, a popular practice among humankind is for males to have consistent, strong, and at-times indiscriminate affection toward females of whatever range would automatically appeal to those males' fancy. I used to be much that way, and I can still be that way to a limited degree early in the interactions with some females upon first meeting. Also, in platonic interactions with males and females, there is often at least a little element of this happening with my psyche. HOWEVER, as interactions proceed, no matter what anyone does in interactions, whether of any gender, any other demographic, of any rank, of any past accomplishments, or whatever, the fact is that at the core level I have the ability to perceive it my duty to REALITY to flip the switch when it becomes evident that I should flip the switch on that. Therefore, no matter how much any combination of beings or any individual might believe himself, herself, itself, or themselves to be entitled to being beyond reproach based on demographics, accomplishments, rank, context, or anything else, I look straight toward THE ABSOLUTE (to whatever degree that IT/HE/SHE/THEY might turn out to be of any given religion(s), any given science(s), and/or any other anything(s), whether best referenced as "G-d," "God," "The Totality of Reality," "The Ultimate Reality," "The Primordial Awakened Consciousness," &c.) such that if the most up-to-date entirety of interaction no longer makes it justified for me to care very thoroughly about the other, then, no matter who the other person is, even a former romantic partner, then I can simply shut down any amount of the affection as if a mechanical device, out of a sincere belief that this is the correct way to serve soteriology. Although some of the people such as a few family members, friends, and acquaintances have found it baffling and perplexing, your pattern has been able to earn a consistently high level with that. To put this another way, although you might perceive that you have done only a modest amount to help my life, I believe and to some degree know that your choices at several key junctures were extraordinarily perfect in terms of helping my life, especially with respect to overcoming obstacles in general, both for my health and for my ability to help other beings.

Although my cousin Alex ({note: text in the forwarded message had "among the two"} who is among the first two on the cc line of this message, out of three total on that cc line) may find it awkward for me to mention it here, this can be illustrated by part of what happened recently during an argument with my mother Ming regarding several things with life in general and differences of choices. In that I said to Mother Ming, "Look, although you have done much to help my life, you have also done much to harm my life. It's not like with my father, who helped my life tremendously--not perfectly, but still tremendously--and who caused only small amounts of harm to my life. With you, in contrast, it's sort of like a company that's only worth $100,000 in balance because it has something like $13 trillion of assets and only $100,000 less than $13 trillion in liabilities." This can be a sample of how people can relate to part of how Stephen R. Covey (1932-2012) and others modeled emotional bank accounts. My late father Maurice A.T. Blair (1931-2015), of course, had what some would consider extreme warping from his combat experiences in Korea and Vietnam, plus the way that many civilians in America acted in portions of the late 1960s to mid-1970s.

*   *   *   *   *

That being said, here is something I have been holding back for years and years from disclosing to the one of you with the name Liza, and which the others of you probably had little or no knowledge regarding, presented as a direct message within this:

Liza, You probably noticed when about one-and-a-half decades ago I notified you by a direct one-to-one message on Facebook that my former upstairs neighbor, Barbara Hawkins (1945-2013), was at times showing signs of not feeling very great with life, given her divorce and other factors, and that she had told me that long ago she was the president of the Duke chapter of Alpha Phi (around the middle of the 1960s). Remembering that you mentioned that you joined Alpha Phi when you and I were discussing Psi Upsilon and other organizations and other stuff, I suggested that maybe you might arrange for a few Alpha Phi Sorority sisters to visit Barbara, perchance to comfort her and help her get better. Although you did not direct message me back about that idea, I have wondered many times in recent years about whether Barbara might have told you what my mother indicated that Barbara told her about the following: Barbara Hawkins perceived Maurice A.T. Blair as having stripped his wife Ming Blair of her femininity, according to accounts and descriptions that Ming Blair told me several times. I have known my mother and my father well enough to be able to tell that the truth is much more intricate than that crude oversimplification. Ming Blair was greatly affected by how her parents were closely involved with the Chinese side of World War II and the Capitalist side of the Chinese Civil War, then fled to Taiwan as part of that Capitalist side. Also, she was affected by many other things besides my father's extremely militaristic influence. When mainstream culture presents things like a son or a daughter considering that descendant's mother as somehow "dearest" or "the primary early source of comfort and support" that is something that to which I can relate by attempting to put myself in their shoes, but it is not at all something that I have felt on any other than the rarest of occasions. Yes, my mother's aneurysm when I was about seven months old and its aftermath are part of why, my mother's growing up in a military family is part of why, my father's militarism was part of why, etc. She sometimes and to some degree cares for people in ways that exhibit significant degrees of femininity, but oftentimes people with sustained and repeated direct contact with her tend to find her to have those tendencies much more curbed than many females. Barbara's idea on this was somewhat overblown in some ways, besides being also a major oversimplification. As this e-mail is part of the sets of forerunners for if and when I might someday compose a full-length autobiography with which to send to literary agents (and perhaps to go unpublished in my lifetime or perhaps go published in my lifetime), here is something insightful that will also possibly disturbing: Ming has told me on multiple occasions, when trying to persuade me to choose to agree more with her on things that I would otherwise disagree, that she believes in an extreme ideal of how descendants would exhibit filial piety, whereas I believe filial piety should be in moderation and should look out for proper tradeoffs with all other types of piety. That is one of the main issues that makes the situation sometimes difficult, besides how she declines to run her online use of accounts, even her email account, shifting all of that responsibility to me since after my father passed on and became no longer available to run my mother's accounts for her, and besides how the nearest known relatives in contact are in California, Hong Kong, and Taiwan, too far away to pick up part of the burden of taking care of her. On another note, my October 1, 2022 e-mail message to you included typing from memory a statement that subtly and unintentionally misstated part of what Dale Carnegie (1888-1955) had stated in *How to Win Friends and Influence People*. From memory, the description was that an editor had told Carnegie that he could tell right away from writings that some people were not going to be popular as writers because they lacked genuine interest in other people, whereas sometime circa mid-2023 I revisited part of that book and found that the actual statement was that an editor had told Carnegie that he could tell right away from writings that some people were not going to be popular as writers because they lacked sufficiently liking people. Something that correcting that characterization makes me think about is that an extraordinary number of times in my life many people have imposed very much on me to avoid liking very many people very much, based on the idea that it would be unethical, impractical, or, for whatever other reason(s), inappropriate. Some of that is readily apparent in much of my writing: over and over again dealing with strong impositions from others to curb or eliminate the liking of people within many ranges.

*   *   *   *   *

Back to addressing all three of the to-line recipients.

Part of the difficulty is exhibited by the following conversational sample, approximating a type of conversation that has happened multiple times. It involves reference to an Asian woman named Sherry, who graduated from college circa 2010, and her father Sam. Bear in mind that it is uncertain to me whether and to what degree my mother might have materially distorted at least one or two elements of something that Sherry had told her.

Ming: You know that Sherry told me that she is so loyal to her father that if he told her to commit suicide, then she would kill herself, no questions asked.

Jim: This is ridiculous! Blind obedience of that kind is way too much! I do not know for sure whether suicide is ever ethical, and if it is, then it is probably only in very limited ranges.

Ming: That's the kind of loyalty that I had toward my parents. You should have that kind of loyalty to ancestors.

Jim: No! I disagree. If my father was still alive, I'm quite sure he would agree with me on this. Maybe the U2 pilot who got shot down in Russia might have better committed suicide as it was what the military guideline for him was in that case in the Cold War, but in the vast majority of cases it seems preposterous to impose on someone that the person go straight into blind obedience to commit suicide on command. This line of thinking is reminiscent of the 1962 version of *The Manchurian Candidate*, which my father and I watched in early 2000 or thereabouts.

*   *   *   *   *

As a last-minute adjustment I decided to add my mother's email address on the cc line. Although she arranges for me to run that account for her, I make sure to be responsible with informing her of any important messages received, and I make sure to only send messages from her account with her consent, knowledge, and direct involvement with the craftsmanship of the messages. It is extraordinarily rare for her to send messages to people, in large part because it takes two people for her to send such a message, with me performing all of her typing, since her arthritis and other factors she uses to be justification to usually completely avoid even touching computer keyboards and computer mice. In this case, I will plan to print out the message and hand her a copy, in order that she can study it at her own pace.

On another note, I have not completely finalized that last will and testament.

It is uncertain whether I might hire Bowker, Kirkus, Kevin Anderson & Associates, or another organization someday for professional editing service(s).

Whatever the case may be, stuff like this can be prime candidates for future nonfiction that I might place within manuscripts to send to agents, whether any of you particularly like it or not. Some parts of the Internet indicate that random people from the general public only get about one manuscript out of six thousand to achieve big-time, mainstream, large-scale publication with major publishers.

I choose to carry virtually no illusions about anyone or anything, because the toughness of life has led me to believe that I generally do not have the right to illusions, except for unintentional and/or inescapable ones, under penalty of nearly unlimited horror from the beyond.

By the way, in a separate communication, I clarified a few months ago to Steve Raynor (who evidently went by "S. T-Bone Raynor" when briefly running for political office in 2022) that instead of "Central Tibetan Authority" in the draft, it should have stated, "Central Tibetan Administration."

Kind Regards, Happy Holidays, and Season's Greetings!

Jim Blair

---------- Forwarded message ----------
From: Maurice Blair
Date: Sun, Dec 22, 2024 at 1:02 AM
Subject: Fwd: A 28 AUG 2024 DRAFT LAST WILL & TESTAMENT, BEFORE ADJUSTMENTS
To: Steve Raynor; Dan Nolan; Ry Pickard

From: Maurice Blair
Date: Wed, Aug 28, 2024 at 3:46 PM
Subject: Re: A 28 AUG 2024 DRAFT LAST WILL & TESTAMENT, BEFORE ADJUSTMENTS
To: Stephen Raynor

Stephen,

In accordance with your request, and providing more than the request for information relevant, here is an extended and edited version of the list in stipulation #11:

—
a. 2% (i.e., one part out of fifty).
International Campaign for Tibet
1825 Jefferson Place NW
Washington, DC 20036
https://savetibet.org/

—
b. 0.2% (i.e., one part out of five hundred).
Duke University Annual Fund
Box 90600
Durham, NC 27708
https://giving.duke.edu/annual-fund/about-the-duke-annual-fund/

—
c. 0.1% (i.e., one part out of one thousand).
Baylor University
Waco, TX 76798
https://www.baylor.edu/

—
d. 0.2% (i.e., one part out of five hundred).
McCombs School of Business
The University of Texas at Austin
2110 Speedway
Austin, TX 78712
https://www.mccombs.utexas.edu/

—
e. Liza Darnton: 1% (i.e., one part out of one hundred). (If she predeceases me, then her next of kin would substitute for her.)

[19]

X handle as of August 2024: @LizaDarnton.

If an executor has difficulty reaching her directly or her closest of next of kin directly, please bear in mind that her father and her brother-in-law were somewhat famous in some circles as of the 2020s, and, therefore, agents of some of her relatives might be helpful with that process.

———

f. The United States of America in such a way as to pay down the national debt and/or build toward a national surplus: 0.2% (i.e., one part out of five hundred). (separate from any tax obligations).

("Gifts to reduce the debt held by the public").

(Cf. https://www.treasurydirect.gov/government/public-debt-reports/gifts/.)

———

g. 0.1% (i.e., one part out of one thousand).
Rice University
6100 Main St.
Houston, TX 77005
rice.edu

———

h. 0.1 % (i.e., one part out of one thousand).
The University of Pennsylvania
Philadelphia, PA 19104
https://www.upenn.edu/

———

i. The Republican Party (of the United States of America): 1% (i.e., one part out of one hundred).
Republican National Committee
310 First Street SE
Washington D C 20003

———

j. The Libertarian Party (of the United States of America): 0.1% (i.e., one part out of one thousand).
Libertarian National Committee
1444 Duke St
Alexandria, VA 22314

———

k. The Democratic Party (of the United States of America): 0.2% (i.e., one part out of five hundred).
Democratic National Committee
430 South Capitol St SE #3
Washington, DC 20003

l. The Green Party (of the United States of America): 0.1% (i.e. one part out of one thousand).
The Green Party of the United States
PO Box 75075
Washington, DC 20013

m. 1% (i.e., one part out of one hundred).
True Buddha Foundation
17110 NE 40th CT, Redmond
WA 98052, USA.

n. Whoever the Director of the Internal Revenue Service Is As of The Time of My Death: 0.01% (i.e., one part out of ten thousand). (Address to be determined).
related addresses as of August 28, 2024:
IRS:
irs.gov.
Department of the Treasury:
treasury.gov.

o. 0.1% (i.e., one part out of one thousand).
The Sheng-Yen Lu Foundation
17102 NE 40th Court Redmond, WA 98052 U.S.A.
https://sylfoundation.org/

p. Frank McDonald II (who was an elementary school classmate in portions of the 1980s in Ysletta Independent School District, and who later connected with me on some portions of online social media): 0.5% (i.e., one part out of two hundred). (If he predeceases me, then his next of kin would substitute for him.)
X handle as of August 2024: @FMcDonald_JDS. As of some portions of the 2020s he worked for Socorro Independent School District.

q. Whoever the Director of the FBI Is As of the Time of My Death: 0.04% (i.e., one part out of two thousand five hundred). related address as of August 28, 2024: Federal Bureau of Investigation
fbi.gov.

r. 0.1% (i.e., one part out of one thousand).

KTLA-TV
5800 Sunset Blvd.
Los Angeles, CA 90028
https://ktla.com/

—

s. 0.1% (i.e., one part out of one thousand).
News Radio KTRH
1233 West Loop South
Suite 725
Houston, TX 77027
https://ktrh.iheart.com/

—

t. 0.2% (i.e., one part out of five hundred).
International Association of Scientologists
4751 Fountain Ave.
Los Angeles, CA 90029, USA
https://iasmembership.org/

—

u. 0.1% (i.e., one part out of one thousand).
Citizens Commission on Human Rights
6616 Sunset Blvd
Los Angeles, California 90028
https://www.cchr.org/

_____

_____

Regards,
Maurice James Blair

On Wed, Aug 28, 2024 at 12:21 PM Stephen Raynor <stephenjamesraynorlaw@gmail.com>
wrote:
Excellent.

On Wed, Aug 28, 2024 at 12:10 PM Maurice Blair <mjblair2956@gmail.com> wrote:
Steve,

Please consider this draft and what some of the proper adjustments might be. BTW, I would
like to see if we might be able to find a way to legally make the adjusted version binding
without adding any more names to it than what it shows. That includes how it painstakingly
uses categories in some cases to sidestep what might otherwise have been the outright
spelling out of additional names.

A 28th Day of August 2024 Draft of What Maurice James Blair (as born an American Citizen by blood in Taiwan on June 14, 1976) Intends for His Last Will and Testament, to be adjusted into Legaleze within a Moderate Amount of Changing After Its Composition

1. All financial accounts that have valid reference to beneficiaries (whether Payable On Death, Transferable On Death, etc.), if any, who are still alive after I die shall go to those beneficiaries in accordance with their registrations, without anyone being able to legally contest otherwise.

2. Any real estate, if any, involved with joint ownership with another person should have my portion become inherited by the surviving person(s), if any, of the joint ownership. In the absence of such joint ownership with any surviving person as of the time of death, such real estate is to go to my closest surviving next of kin. If there is a tie for whom the claim to "closest surviving next of kin" would be, then it should go pro rata on an equal basis to each tying claimant. (Any subsequent descriptions in this document to "closest surviving next of kin" are also subject to this provision.) (For certain contingencies of disputes, please refer to stipulation #9.)

3. Any automobile, if any, of my sole ownership should go to the closest surviving next of kin.

4. Real estate, if any, of my sole ownership should go to the closest surviving next of kin.

5. Automobile(s), if any, of joint ownership should have my portion go to the surviving person(s), if any, of the joint ownership.

6. If I own shares of Synapsid Revelations Press Corporation at the time of my death, then those shares should go to Liza Darnton (who attended a philosophy class as one of my classmates in the Spring Semester of 1995, and who later became part of my LinkedIn network concomitant with my later becoming part of her LinkedIn network). With those shares, of course, go the royalties on any books registered for that corporation to receive royalties. (Of course, with this goes access to the safe deposit box(es), if any, registered for that corporation. However, such deposit box(es) should already have in them notes making clear which items within them are property of Synapsid Revelations Press Corporation and which items within them are my property. Therefore, there should be care to make sure that the appropriate items within those boxes go to the proper recipients; see stipulation #10 of this list.) If Liza Darnton predeceases me, then her next of kin are to receive those shares in her place.

7. Liza Darnton is also to receive the copyrights to the books published by Synapsid Revelations Press Corporation with myself as the author. If she predeceases me, then her next of kin are to receive those copyrights in her place.

8. If I have more than one residence at which I keep my nonautomobile personal property, then the executors should discuss with appropriate persons which of such property was solely possessed by me, which such property was jointly owned with others, etc. Any solely-owned property of that type should go to whomever else, if anyone, was a resident primarily of the place where it was at the time of my death. In the absence of anyone having primarily resided at such a place, my next of kin should negotiate among themselves who should inherit what among those items. If such next of kin should enter a dispute about who should inherit what with that, then they should face off in a nonphysically-threatening duel contest in their determination of at least one competition among 1) tennis (via a three-set match), 2) table tennis (via an old-school first to reach twenty-one points contest), 3) chess (via a match consisting of at least four games), 4) poker (by five card draw with a traditional 52-card modern deck, with officials carefully preventing anything other than a fair competition of it), 5) flipping a coin (of exactly or almost exactly 50%-50% chances for heads and tails), observed officially and adjudicated by the executor of the will if the executor is not among the disputants. If the executor of the will is among the disputants, then the next of kin of Frank McDonald II should serve as the official observer and judge. If Frank McDonald II is still alive as of that time, then he should determine which of his next of kin would serve in that capacity. If the determined person does not feel qualified to be such an observer and judge, then that person shall be assigned to designate anyone appropriate of that person's choice to be the objective third party to serve in that role. If the next person up does not feel qualified, then that person is to designate another person. This process can proceed through whatever number of people would be needed to arrive at a resolution. If the executor of the estate determines there to have occurred too many rounds of designated people sidestepping considering themselves qualified, then the executor could call off that process, replacing it with a simple resolution in which any basically competent and objective adult can observe a simple drawing of a single Tarot card by each dueling person from a randomly shuffled Oswald Wirth Tarot Deck, with high card winning, in accordance with the following basis in this case: 1) Each Major Arcana card outranks any of the Minor Arcana cards. 2) Card XXI of the Major Arcana ranks highest, and the other 77 cards proceed in rank in descending order, with Card XX ranking second, with Card I as the penultimate in the order (i.,e., second to last / second to lowest in rank among those) and Card 0 as the lowest in that arcana. 3) Of the Minor Arcana the Aces rank highest, Kings second highest, Queens third, Knights fourth, and Pages fifth, Ten ranking sixth, and the remainder proceeding in descending order, with the Deuces last / lowest ranking. 4) In this case the four suits shall be given a ranking (in case of what would otherwise be an Ace-vs.-Ace tie, a 10-vs.-10 tie, etc.) of Swords highest ranked, Cups second ranked, Wands third ranked, and Coins fourth ranked. Therefore, the Two (i.e., Deuce) of Coins would be the lowest ranking card in that setup, whereas XXI. The World would be the highest ranking card in that setup.

9. If any disputes among heirs and/or attempted heirs occur and appear to otherwise be headed for costly legal disputes in a court of law or multiple courts of law regarding the carrying out of any potential disputes other than those described for resolution in stipulation #8, then, rather than fully utilizing such courts, the dispute resolution technique outlined in stipulation #8 should be utilized for them.

10. As part of facilitating stipulation #6, prior to separating which property within Synapsid Revelations Press Corporation's safe deposit box(es), if any, should go to whom, any person opening the box(es) should utilize sufficient videorecording and/or presence of witnesses to facilitate reasonable confidence among affected parties that the proceedings are happening properly. This might require extra care in negotiating with the bank(s) and/or others exactly how the proceedings can happen.

11. If as of the time of my death I have any nonretirement (i.e., bank accounts, brokerage accounts, etc. other than IRAs, etc.) financial accounts that lack any designated beneficiary, such that the financial institutions have no clear guidance on distribution/transfer upon my death, and/or if there are any nonretirement financial accounts for which any and all designated beneficiary/beneficiaries is/are already deceased prior to my death, then the distribution of those fund should be in accordance with the percentages detailed as follows:
a. International Campaign for Tibet: 2% (i.e., one part out of fifty).
b. Duke University: 0.2% (i.e., one part out of five hundred).
c. Baylor University: 0.1% (i.e., one part out of one thousand).
d. The University of Texas at Austin: 0.2% (i.e., one part out of five hundred).
e. Liza Darnton: 1% (i.e., one part out of one hundred). (If she predeceases me, then her next of kin would substitute for her.)
f. The United States of America in such a way as to pay down the national debt and/or build toward a national surplus: 0.2% (i.e., one part out of five hundred). (separate from any tax obligations).
g. Rice University: 0.1% (i.e., one part out of one thousand).
h. The University of Pennsylvania (at Philadelphia): 0.1 % (i.e., one part out of one thousand).
i. The Republican Party (of the United States of America): 1% (i.e., one part out of one hundred).
j. The Libertarian Party (of the United States of America): 0.1% (i.e., one part out of one thousand).
k. The Democratic Party (of the United States of America): 0.2% (i.e., one part out of five hundred).
l. The Green Party (of the United States of America): 0.1% (i.e. one part out of one thousand).
m. True Buddha School Foundation: 1% (i.e., one part out of one hundred). (This portion should probably be delivered by check to it, because one time in 2023 I did what I thought was a wire transfer to it, but it turned out that they counted it as a personal gift to Grand

Master Sheng-Yen Lu himself, therefore telling me that the wire transfer would not count as a tax deductible donation.)

n. Whoever the Director of the Internal Revenue Service Is As of The Time of My Death: 0.01% (i.e., one part out of ten thousand).

o. The Sheng-Yen Lu Foundation: 0.1% (i.e., one part out of one thousand).

p. Frank McDonald II (who was an elementary school classmate in portions of the 1980s, and who later connected with me on some portions of online social media): 0.5% (i.e., one part out of two hundred).

q. Whoever the Director of the FBI Is As of the Time of My Death: 0.04% (i.e., one part out of two thousand five hundred).

r. The television station KTLA: 0.1% (i.e., one part out of one thousand).

s. The radio station KTRH: 0.1% (i.e., one part out of one thousand).

t. International Association of Scientologists: 0.2% (i.e., one part out of five hundred).

u. Citizens Commison on Human Rights: 0.1% (i.e., one part out of one thousand).

v. My Next of Kin: The remaining residual (i.e., 93%, in other words, ninety-three parts out of one hundred). (However, portions of that may need to go toward paying taxes.)

12. The United States Federal Bureau of Investigation (hereafter referred to as "the FBI") is to be granted by my cellphone and email account providers (if any) full access to my cellphone and email records. The FBI is to also determine which portion(s) if any of that information would be appropriate to disclose to my next of kin and/or other persons. If the FBI no longer exists at the time of my death, then the United States Central Intelligence Agency (hereafter referred to as "the CIA") is to receive such access in its place. If neither the FBI nor the CIA exist as of the time of my death, then the executor of the estate is to decide to whom access to those records should be granted.

13. The Central Tibetan Authority (hereafter referred to as "the CTA") is to be granted by my social media providers full access to my social media accounts. The CTA is also to determine which portion(s) if any of that information would be appropriate to disclose to my next of kin and/or other persons. If the CTA no longer exists as of that time or declines to obtain such access, then such access is to be granted to Duke University. If Duke University no longer exists as of that time or declines to obtain such access, then such access is to be granted to The University of Texas at Austin. If The University of Texas at Austin no longer exists as of that time or declines to obtain such access, then the executor of the estate is to decide to whom access to those records should be granted.

14. If any retirement accounts lack designated beneficiaries, then 2% of them are to go to International Campaign for Tibet, 3% of them are to go to Liza Darnton (or, if she predeceases me, then her next of kin), 1% to Frank McDonald II (or, if he predeceases me, then his next of kin), and 94% of them are to go to my next of kin.

[26]

15. My next of kin and whichever organizations might obtain access to informative accounts via stipulation #12 and/or stipulation #13 are to be reasonably cooperative with Liza Darnton (or her next of kin if she predeceases me) and my next of kin, in order to facilitate interactions helpful toward the future of sentient beings. If they decide to decline to cooperate at all, then the beings with whom they decline to cooperate are to use any and all means they deem appropriate to convert that lack of cooperation into usefully becoming part of facilitating interactions helpful toward the future of sentient beings.

16. If the telephone provider(s), email providers, and social media providers wind up obstructing the fulfilment of stipulation #12 and/or stipulation #13 and/or stipulation #15, then anyone named and/or otherwise identified by this will shall hereby be encouraged to use any and all means deemed appropriate to help foster the future of the enlightenment of sentient beings.

17. My next of kin are to inherit any copyrights to which I am both the copyright office claimant and the publisher (in contrast with the items described by stipulation #7). They are also to inherit any royalties from those works.

18. The executor is to make sure to facilitate for the fulfilment of stipulations #6, #7, and #17 to include proper dissemination of computer files supportive of the future processes, if any, involved with the related publishing activities.

19. If the heirs who receive in accordance with stipulations #6, #7, and #17 sell rights to any stories to be converted into movies, then they are hereby encouraged, though not required, to arrange that some consultation with at least five persons in total and/or at least two organizations in total from the list consisting of the following would be involved with that process: The list from stipulation #11 plus The Church of Jesus Christ, Scientist (also referred to as the main Christian Science organization), The Methodist Church, The Drukpa Church of Nepal, The Philadelphia Seminar on Christian Origins, Houston Zen Center, Holocaust Museum Houston, The Smithsonian Institution (as was located in the District of Columbia as of 2024), and, last but not least, the Tibetan Buddhist Rimé Institute (as was located in Australia as of 2024).

20. Anyone who might ever encounter this will and/or its draft hereby receives a proclamation of encouragement to do whatever such persons and organizations might be able to do to help with the soteriology with which to transform a given reality into a better reality.

———————————————————————————————————————

Regards,

Maurice James Blair

P.S. Please keep in some version of the extra verbiage in 11(m), because it opens the door to the possibility that, even though I choose much loyalty to TBS, if the IRS deems it appropriate to audit and argue with TBS about the procedure by which TBS managed the record keeping aftermath of that wire transfer (and how it presumably has in recent years managed the record keeping of similar such wire transfers), then I can fulfill my duty to REALITY to alert the IRS about that situation. That is also part of why I insist on 11(n) being adjacent to 11(m), to make extra sure that this opens the door to any relevant, appropriate, extra consideration of options by any affected organizations. Also, I reserve the right to accelerate the alerting of people and organizations about this or whatever else, by if I, for example, copy this message to becoming part of some yet-to-be-determined future publication, devoid of identifying which attorney and law office to whom I am sending it (for your privacy). Alternatively, with a similar m.o., I might copy some excerpts of it to some yet-to-be-determined future publication(s). I trust how TBS personnel responded to me about that situation, yet I remembered that a tax CPE course years ago indicated some preacher attempted an in-person method similar to that online procedure, and a tax court later ruled him to have received those payments not as tax-free gifts from the congregation, but as taxable income to himself.

--

STEPHEN JAMES RAYNOR
Attorney and Counselor at Law

D2: Comments on D1:
Redacted screenshots involving this appear later in this literary work. Also, the transcription in D1 included correcting in one spot to use the phrase "her place" where my email message had used the phrase "my place." The unintentional typo's origin may have been related to how I have often in portions of early April 1995 and portions of June 19, 2022 to the time of the publication of this book valued Liza's well-being more than I have valued my own well-being. I am honest with myself that the chances that she and I even meet again in this life are slim, yet I think and feel and know that she has thoroughly earned my respect and very thoroughly healed me through her combined total sum of choices, actions, ways of showing initiative, and ways of showing restraint in terms of how it has affected me. My friend Frank McDonald II, my fraternity brother Marcus Padow, a few of my family members, and a few others have had very favorable effects on me, yet, somehow, that philosophy classmate Liza has been at a whole other level!
   (Cf. Portions of *The Science, Religion, Politics, and Cards Trilogy*, which consists of *Science, Religion, Politics, and Cards* (2023), *Alternative Beginnings and Endings of All Things: Science, Religion, Politics, and Cards, Hypervolume II* (2024), and *Simplicity, Intricacy, and Beyond* (2024).)

Part II of this Prelude and/or Trailer:

A. Several Perspectives on The Relationship Between North Americans and Buddhism, Other Beings' Relationships With Buddhism, and My Relationship With Buddhism

1. Here is part of a February 26, 2022 three-page autobiography that I composed mainly in order to send to True Buddha School medium-high-ranking monk Master Lian Yuan as part of my then-attempt to apply for professional employment by that organization as a member of its clergy / sangha, adjusted for font and alignment consistency with this book:

From June 1976 to September 1982, my residences included Taiwan, South Korea, New Hampshire, and Montana. In September 1982, my nuclear family moved from Millcreek (in Park County, near Livingston, Montana) to Texas, arriving in El Paso. My residences since then included: El Paso (SEP 1982 – JUN 1994), Charlotte, NC (JUN 1994 to AUG 1994 and portions of AUG 1994 to mid-1995), Durham, NC (portions of AUG 1994 to mid-1995 and more completely from mid-1995 to JAN 1999), Houston, TX (JAN 1999-mid-2000, FEB 2001-APR 2001, and mid-2002-to-the-present), and Austin, TX (mid-2000-FEB 2001, APR 2001-mid-2002).

Here are highlights of some empowerments of Maurice James Blair as of the time of composing this historical record:

- The legacy of MJB's paternal grandfather's research into Russian Occultist P.D. Ouspensky's life and works
- The legacy of MJB's maternal family's involvement with Generalissimo Chiang Kai Shek and related persons and organizations
- The legacy of MATB's service to the U.S. Army, especially combat in Asia in the 1950s and 1960s
- The legacy of DAB's service to the U.S. Army, especially combat in Europe in the 1910s
- Various empowerments through MJB's official affiliation with True Buddha School since October 2003
- The legacy of various Blair forefathers traceable to 1600s Scotland
- Maurice James Blair's various research and development, including weaving together technologies and other methods from a multitude of sources and in some cases going beyond anything "given" by others

---

2. Note: "MATB" in that context is a reference to my father, and "DAB" in that context is a reference to his father.

---

3. Here is another font-and-alignment-adjusted portion of the aforementioned three-page:

Regarding Vajrayana Buddhism and Extremely Similar Sets of Technologies and Methods and Such: Although I received empowerments via True Buddha School, I also received blessings to chant and visualize and otherwise coordinate via a CD-ROM I purchased in connection with Geshe Galek Chodak performing and participated in mantra projects involving Khandro.net in connection with some expressions of The Karmapa and related beings. Master Lian Yuan of True Buddha School and I discussed some elements of this and other Buddhism-versus-Buddhism perspectives in middle portions of the first decade of the Twenty-First Century.

4. Next, behold a message that I posted to LinkedIn at about 6:47 A.M. CST on December 18, 2024, after meditating on huge amounts of Anti-Buddhist sentiment having been evident in several parts of American society as of the November 2004 to December 17, 2024 period:

If your interpretation of THE QUR'AN, THE TANAKH, and/or THE BIBLE has led you to hatred toward THE SACRED BOOKS OF THE EAST, VOL. XLIX, then this will probably not turn out well for you unless and until you let go of that hatred. Such letting go may open the floodgates to a more enlightened approach toward any and all texts, videos, audios, and, last but not least, sentient beings.

5. Consider how page 426 of *Alternative Beginnings and Endings of All Things: Science, Religion, Politics, and Cards, Hypervolume II* (2024 C.E.) mentions that some have said that Shakyamuni Buddha presented to the public the idea, "Hatred does not cease hatred, but by Love alone is healed." That served as an approximation of several translations of one of the most famous lines from *The Dhammapada* (c. 5th or 6th century B.C.E.).

6. Although it may seem unusual, in some cases offering direct criticism of a criticism can be helpful with getting people to understand things better. This can in such cases be true to a major degree in the medium run whether one side comes around to agreeing with the other side, the two sides choose to agree to disagree, or the two sides outright fight. On at least one occasion in mid-2024, the aforementioned Johnny Ross II and I shared a discussion that essentially unfolded as follows:

Ross: What's the book about?

Blair: A whole bunch of stuff, mainly pushing back against problems in order to give people a better chance at making life better. *Alternative Beginnings and Endings of All Things*. The title communicates much of its emphasis. Besides including records of actual back-and-forth e-mail messages and other forms of dialogue, some of it takes a deep dive into how people with wrong-headed ways of thinking about me can be dead wrong, and it then demonstrates how and why those ways of thinking are wrong, giving a path toward becoming more accurate with thinking about me. It shows some of how they could become people with right-headed ways of thinking about me.

Ross: So a bunch of it is just you talking to yourself.

Blair: No! Did you even listen to what I just told you?!

Ross: That's what that sounded like to me.

Blair: Look, the wrong-headed ways of thinking about me on those are not what I think about myself, because I know the refutations of them. Also, I demonstrate the refutations. Instead of me talking to myself, those parts present ways that some other people might sometimes stupidly and inaccurately think of me and ways that they might change over to intelligently and accurately thinking of me. That serves as part of accuracy in general.

* * *

Another argument that he and I had several times concerned the bar fight that I described both in that May 2024 book and in the December 2023 online article "Why I Support Tibetan Sky Burial." Although John Ross II was not there to witness the fight, his analysis of the facts I presented led to him believing me to be primarily to blame for it, whereas I have told him and others that I believe the main blame for the fight can be attributed to much of the American society of the early 21st century failing to sufficiently respect Buddhism in general, Himalayan culture in general, and reasonably-enlightened mindsets in general.

For more about this please consider exploring the free online flipbook *Impact* (published on 1/1/2024; still available at the https://mixam.com/share/659351615dddc94c958bb985 URL as of January 7, 2025) and/or a print copy of that intended-for-free-distribution book and/or Part Four of Chapter Six of *Alternative Beginnings and Endings of All Things: Science, Religion, Politics, and Cards, Hypervolume II*.

* * *

Despite the fact that I went into those discussions with John Ross II and had presented in that very book what some would consider major steelman defenses against those mindsets against Buddhism, against the First Amendment, against my family, against me, and against the book itself, eventually Kirkus Reviews completed a review of that Hypervolume II book, and, lo and behold, the anonymous reviewer they contracted evidently went into the same sorts of traps into which Ross had fallen.

Although the contractual arrangement between Kirkus Reviews and indie authors (i.e., authors who used independent publishing to reach the public) has several legal restrictions, both to restrict the authors and to restrict the reviewing organization, it is clearly legal and ethical for me to copy the entire review to part of this book, then copy to this book portions of *Alternative Beginnings and Endings of All Things* that some would consider to have strongly and preemptively fought back against those mentalities. Others might already be hell-bent against one or more of the affiliations, clearly-stated main ideas, or other expressions or aspects of that book at an impersonal level, thereby considering the book to confirm the review to a major degree rather than preemptively refuting it. Some of those others might combine that with something against me personally, too. This is not way too much of a reason for concern, as the patterns of sowing, reaping, and revelation will hopefully force those on every side of every disagreement everywhere in the long run to have to shape up or ship out with respect to levels of reality beyond the ordinary world. That is, whether and to whatever degree that it might involve one religious and/or scientific conceptualization of the beyond, another religious and/or scientific conceptualization of the beyond, and/or whatever else might turn out to be completely true.

A massive compendium of the author's thoughts on society, religion, and other topics.

In this follow-up to *Science, Religion, Politics, and Cards* (2023), Blair presents his thoughts on a wide variety of subjects, from incidents in history to aspects of religion and spirituality. Despite the author's attempts to broaden his focus, virtually everything in these pages remains intensely personal, oriented entirely around Blair's own thoughts and experiences, often delivered in fragments and without any context. Long breakdowns of various religious concepts jostle against hand-drawn alternate Tarot cards and single-paragraph reviews of movies (about 2023's *Indiana Jones and the Dial of Destiny*, Blair enigmatically writes, "Extraordinarily expressive virtually any way a person can behold it *if the viewer does not feel jolted by implications*"). The prose often reads oddly, as when the author describes the Oneida Colony as existing in "something like the Nineteenth Century" (it existed in the 19th century) in "something like upstate New York" (it was located in upstate New York) "an extremely long time ago" (it ended in 1875). Many of his reminiscences included here are abbreviated, incomplete, or jarringly self-incriminating. When someone asks Blair a pro forma question about what sets him apart from other people, his response is, "That is on a need-to-know basis, and you don't need to know it at this time. If someday a situation happens such that you wind up needing to know that, then maybe you will wind up knowing it then."

At the beginning of this book, Blair includes a note advising his readers that they need not have read its preceding volume to appreciate this present work. Although this is true in terms of continuity of content, familiarity with the first book would at least prepare the reader for the hyperactive delivery, abundance of material, and near-complete incoherence that characterize this project. The text essentially reads like an 800-page private diary, consisting mostly of transcribed notes from the author to himself. In 2010, for instance, he attends Olivia Newton-John's keynote speech for Integrative Health in Westchester, Pennsylvania. Rather than describe the speech (or include a transcript), Blair reproduces the thoughts he recorded while listening "as an out-of-state visitor observing the proceedings, though remaining silent except for minimal small talk with attendees"; in other words, pages of jottings that are incomprehensible to anybody on Earth except for himself. The huge majority of the book is similarly circumscribed by the author's solipsism. Some of the pages have illustrations by the author (and plenty of typos, like "I deliberately budded in"), and almost all of them are filled with telegraphic bits and pieces of nonsense or windy, aimless prose like, "However, I believe that there is potential value at times with if a human being, after killing an animal, rather than choosing to seek to fully eat that animal, chooses to leave some portion of the remains for whichever scavenger animals might happen to come along and eat that remainder of the remains." Readers will find precious little to latch onto here.

A bewildering assortment of thoughts and half-thoughts about dozens of subjects.

—*Kirkus Reviews*

(Cf. https://www.kirkusreviews.com/book-reviews/maurice-james-blair/alternative-beginnings-and-endings-of-all-things/ as accessed on December 17, 2024 and January 7, 2025.)

One way to respond to that review would be to quote the second paragraph of p. 313 of that book: "For those who fall into thinking about all of Buddhism in ways paralleling what F. Max Müller described as even many intelligent people being prone to thinking about *The Vajracchedika Sutra* as nonsensical, the huge factors that they fail to anticipate in relationship with Buddhism could lead to all sorts of brutal consequences. Many of the consequences are things to which they may find themselves repeatedly blind, deaf, and unfeeling, unless and until they wise up and wake up to recognizing the patterns."

Another way would be to point toward how in the wake of the review, I conducted a focused campaign to rectify the impact of the review, which eventually led to a December 23, 2024 e-mail message (primarily to one Kirkus Reviews employee and secondarily to an array of other recipients) in which I stated clearly, coherently, and unequivocally that both major U.S. political parties of the early 21st century are potentially expendable, whereas soteriology is central to the long run well-being of sentient beings.

7. Consider a passage shared almost identically by the article "Why I Support Tibetan Sky Burial" https://www.linkedin.com/pulse/why-i-support-tibetan-sky-burial-maurice-blair-ckbqc as accessed on 9 DEC 2023 & 7 JAN 2025), pp. 61-62 of *Impact* (2024), & p. 89 of *Alternative Beginnings and Endings of All Things: Science, Religion, Politics, and Cards, Hypervolume II* (2024), with this manifestation utilizing subtle hybridization of prior minor formatting differences:

A light-skinned woman said to a white man something very much like, "I've heard that if you hunt an animal, then you really should eat all its remains, out of respect for the life that you have taken from that animal."

I deliberately budded in with something like, "Although there could be much truth to that view, there are other ways of dealing with these kinds of issues. I respect how various people, including Ted Nugent, have presented the practice that you just mentioned. However, I believe that there is potential value at times with if a human being, after killing an animal, rather than choosing to seek to fully eat that animal, chooses to leave some portion of the remains for whichever scavenger animals might happen to come along and eat that remainder of the remains.

"*Furthermore, there is a practice of Himalayan sky burial, in which priests can prepare a human corpse such that it can nourish animals who come along.* I support the legalization of Himalayan sky burial in the United States of America, including in Texas."

Comment: The hybrid of "butting in" and "budding in" here could be thought of as, "Maurice James Blair considered Vajrayana Buddhist strength to justify jumping into the conversation, whether those there would consider it unjustified butting in or justified promoting the budding of enlightenment."

B. Several Ideas about Beings and Their Perceptions Regarding the Relationships Between Each Portion of Politics and Religion with Each Other Portion of Politics and Religion

"This modesty in a sect is perhaps a singular instance in the history of mankind, every other sect supposing itself in possession of all truth, and that those who differ are so far in the wrong ; like a man traveling in foggy weather, those at some distance before him on the road he sees wrapped up in the fog, as well as those behind him, and also the people in the fields on each side, but near him all appears clear, tho' in truth he is as much in the fog as any of them." —Benjamin Franklin, *The Autobiography of Benjamin Franklin* (1791 / 1793 / &c. / a work that has been reprinted and re-published in many formats, e.g., p. 100 of ISBN 978-1612930138, Tribeca Books, 2011)

"A problem with much of modern civilization is something that has been around in civilizations for eons, namely that few people and groups seem to exhibit much, if any, of the modesty that Benjamin Franklin praised the Dunkers as having demonstrated. Perhaps topping the list of those manifesting that problem have been the most toxic, closed-minded, extremist members of the Democrat Party of the 2000-2024 quarter century. Troublesome also have been the most toxic, closed-minded, extremist members of the Republican Party of the 2000-2024 quarter century, but, to my experience, there is much more of that toxic blindly brainwashed, groupthink, overly self-righteous ignorance among Democrats than among Republicans during that period. All political parties should work on getting better, lest they lose the mandate of heaven and go extinct." —M. James Blair, the author of this book, composed that for inclusion here in *Shape Up or Ship Out: A Message to All Political Parties* (2025)

Reporting A Suspicious 01 FEB 2022 Occurrence

Maurice Blair ███████████████████   Mon, Dec 23, 2024 at 3:33 PM
To: Liza Darnton ████████████████████, Dan Nolan ███████@kirkus.com>, Ry Pickard ████████@kirkus.com>, Jason
Peltz <jason.peltz@bartlitbeck.com>, David Grann ███████████████████, Steve Raynor
████████████████████████ , info@wealthenhancement.com, Michael Kelsheimer <mkelsheimer@grayreed.com>,
dkroll@grayreed.com, jreed@grayreed.com, Rose Rodriguez ████████████████████ , Johnny Ross
████████████████████ , Ming Blair ████████████████ , Alex Tse ████████████████████ , Jennifer Wei
████████████████████ , info@harriscountygop.com, hpd.communityaffairs@houstonpolice.org, Marcus Padow
████████████████

---------- Forwarded message ---------
From: **Maurice Blair** ████████████████████████
Date: Mon, Dec 23, 2024 at 10:59 AM
Subject: Reporting A Suspicious 01 FEB 2022 Occurrence
To: Marcus Padow ████████████████
Cc: Dan Nolan ████████████████ , Ry Pickard ████████████████████

Marcus,

In the evening of February 1, 2022 I was dining in Austin, Texas, when an unusual elderly man walked in. Since I recently sent you one copy each of *Alternative Beginnings and Endings of All Things: Science, Religion, Politics, and Cards, Hypervolume II* (2024), *The Dimetrodons, the Dorians, and the Modern World, Synapsid Critical Edition* (2024) (hereafter in this message referred to as TDTDATMSCE), and additional books as a gift, I can simplify part of this communique by mentioning that the Billy mentioned in part of the epilogue of TDTDATMSCE was precisely that man.

Something truly suspicious that I omitted from TDTDATMSCE, yet regarding which I informed the CIA (assuming that they received the items arranged with which to inform them of it), is as follows:

That specific Billy, who also went by "Billy Q.," within about ten or fifteen minutes of both first meeting a construction industry entrepreneur (whom to the best of memory was named Rick, and whom this message will sometimes refer to as Rick) and first meeting me, informed both that construction businessman and me an allegation that he, Billy Q. was a CIA agent.

Furthermore, he flashed a badge that purported to be a CIA badge. Now, this was extraordinarily suspicious, as, to the best of my knowledge, CIA agents would either never or virtually never conduct themselves in this way. That being said, I chose the very polite, very agreeable path of not daring even once to speak out loud my suspicion that he might be illegally impersonating a CIA officer.

I do not remember any specific extra identification of letters from his badge, beyond that it seemed to corroborate that "Billy Q." could be an appropriate variation of his name. One of the things that seemed extra suspicious was that he at some stage indicated that he and a female CIA officer had traveled in foreign countries in such a way that the female partner had sometimes quickly proceeded to execute foreign citizens in informal settings for showing modest amounts of disrespect and suspiciousness. "Trigger happy," as some might say.

Later, Billy arranged with Rick and me that all three of us would go by our own vehicles in a caravan over to a nearby bar. At the bar, at some point he asked Rick to consider in a hypothetical in which Billy might instruct him to shoot me dead someday whether Rick might be willing and able to execute me in such circumstances. He mentioned this casually, in passing, with me right there at the table with him and Rick as he said that. It was one of those ambiguous things in which it is unclear how much, if any, is meant in humor, and how much, if any, is meant in seriousness. At least one or two of our fraternity brothers mentioned before that my Psi U. big brother Evan Henkin was often inscrutable in terms of, "Is he joking or is he serious?" and this seemed along similar lines. I responded, to some degree playfully and with good gallows humor and to some degree seriously, that I was not very sure if Rick would succeed if setting out to kill me by shooting. Although I could go into much more detail, I will stop here and segue into related topics.

As you probably remember, shortly before I got involved with becoming a patient of the psychiatric industry, in fact, before I initially walked into CAPS at Duke to find out what sort of evaluation they might give to me, you and I had a peculiar conversation. It proceeded as follows, from what I remember, and, unless something very bizarre has happened and/or you somehow do not remember it, you probably remember it having been essentially identical to the following account.

Approximately late September or early October 1996 was when that happened. It was in a group setting involving the Chi Delta Chapter of Psi Upsilon Fraternity. This might be splicing an element from two different conversations or it might be essentially matching just one conversation.

Jim: With my having difficulty concentrating on classes lately, I think I have paranoid schizophrenia.

Marcus: You don't have schizophrenia. I studied this sort of stuff, and schizophrenics typically have things like thinking that they have scissors for hands. You are not that extreme with your difficulties. Yes, you have overbearing parents and other problems, but I do not believe that you have schizophrenia.

After that, some time went by and I continued to struggle with the classes. One book I omitted to send you within the gift (which I am uncertain of whether you have received or will ever receive, although records indicated that it was received successfully) is *Science, Religion, Politics, and Cards* (2023), which discusses in greater depth much of what transpired. That being said, I ordered to send complimentary copies of it directly to the FBI itself soon after clearing the hurdles of the online publishing aggregator. Therefore, I do not know whether or not you have already accessed it. A brief synopsis of part of that is that I was molested in approximately the November 1981 to February 1982 period one day in Taiwan by a male stranger, and I believe that experiencing that was a major contributor to how I later had mental concentration issues and wound up a psychiatric patient for a while. Once I extracted myself from the psychiatric industry, thereby changing from a psychiatric patient into becoming a former psychiatric patient, it seemed clear to me that either the single most critical element or one of the most critical elements of that extraction was overcoming the confusion from the child molestation experience perpetrated by an adult male stranger.

Although people can energize with esoteric consciousness and/or zen consciousness unlimited variations of idea structures to have at least a microscopic degree of truth, in many contexts some ideas carry much more energy than others, and there can be much controversy. Having stated that, I believe that your first reaction to when I attempted to diagnose myself a paranoid schizophrenic, a reaction in which you expressed a belief that the root problems were not schizophrenia or another of the most dread of psychiatric diagnoses, was the correct one. Oddly enough, when I went in for evaluation, even without my--to the best of my memory--saying out loud to them a suggestion of paranoid schizophrenia, that was the first main diagnosis that they ended up saying out loud to me. At a basic level, the most intuitive and accurate interpretation seems to me to be that the trauma and confusion from various incidents had weighed too much and resulted in temporary impairment of mind, later some paranormal and/or paranormalesque experiences occurred, though not primarily attributable to any disruption of the core functioning of mind, and, with sufficient paying my dues through all sorts of methods, I was able to free myself from enough of the problems to function reasonably well often enough to stay long-term fully extracted out of psychiatric industry patienthood.

Nevertheless, it has become abundantly clear from some interactions in recent years that it might have been a huge mistake to walk into Counseling and Psychological Services (CAPS) about five weeks into the Fall Semester of 1996. If I were to someday experience a much more extreme time loop than the one described in the epilogue of TDTDATMWSCE, that is, if I were to experience a new time loop so extreme that I were teleported / transfigured to just before walking into CAPS back there about 3/4 the way into 1996 C.E., then I would probably opt to walk into the Dean's office and discuss withdrawing from classes without getting any psychiatric evaluation. After that, I would work toward sorting things out, leaving psychiatrists either as a last resort or nearly a last resort. However, I respect that different people have different situations and that some people sometimes probably do face situations in which it is appropriate for them to get psychiatric evaluations.

Part of why I state this is that the stigma with having ever been a patient of that industry is evidently extreme, based on such evidence as the choices that the Kirkus review of *Science, Religion, Politics, and Cards* and the Kirkus review of *Alternative Beginnings and Endings of All Things* had in terms of what to present, what to sidestep, and what to emphasize.

The epitome of much of this is how some major percentage of people model the controversies on the locked-into-being-wrong the way that some people fall into a trap with, as described on pp. 382-386 of *Alternative Beginnings and Endings of All Things*. That was a way in which Justin Haynes demonstrated being trapped for a while later on, before I succeeded in helping him to succeed in snapping out of it. Cf. *A 24 October 2024 Open Letter to the United States Congress* (2024), pp. 7-42, 44-57. [Later in this message, this paragraph shall be referred to as "TEOMOT," an acronym for "The epitome of much of this..."]

Some might point out any of a host of things to question my credibility as a witness, yet I believe that a reasonably holistic evaluation would indicate that are strong arguments in favor of my credibility.

Since there are possibilities of questioning my credibility in connection with this and I found the recent Kirkus review of *Alternative Beginnings and Endings of All Things* insulting in terms of being on exactly the wrong side of the very issue referenced in TEOMOT, I tentatively plan on also forwarding to you, with them on the cc line again, one more message after this.

This also ties into the robbery from September 9, 2022. Its aftermath can beg the question of why the Houston Police Department did not more vigorously pursue evidence when they otherwise could have done so. The trail of my blood near the apartment unit where one man had threatened me with a gun and another man had hit me over the head with a pipe would have probably been easy for them to find had they prioritized it and gone over there to look. Yet another insult to the entirety of my life and the reality of my entire family!!

I have decided to include a pdf of the message from a little while ago with this message, for convenient reference.

As expressed in some ways directly and in other ways between the lines in the next message--if it actually happens and you actually wind up receiving it--I still respect the Kirkus review that was profoundly insulting toward the reality of my life, the reality of my entire family's life, and the spiritual conglomerate (of Jeet Kune Do, Esotericism, Buddhism, Modern Physics, etc.) that has worked well for me in recent decades because: 1) It works well as comedy. 2) Between the lines, people in the know--whether they personally know me or any other one specific individual sentient being or not--can see through several features in a manner actually assisted by some of the reviewer's choices of what to point out (especially the "need-to-know" reference). 3) It alerted me to the value of fighting back more thoroughly against any and all who are causing problems.

Although I only practice Noahidism part of the time and to some degree, it could probably make it extra appropriate to, given portions of your background as of the mid-1990s emphasizing portions of the Jewish-and-Noahidist complementary ranges, give you in this season the ensuing greeting: Happy Hanukkah!

Jim Blair

 **202412230843.pdf**
209K

Fw: [EXTERNAL EMAIL] - _____, , or regarding "Form 3X" or "not Form 3X"

From Jim Blair ████████████████████

Date Mon 12/23/2024 8:43 AM

To Marcus Padow <████████@fbi.gov>; Ry Pickard <████████@kirkus.com>; Dan Nolan <████████@kirkus.com>

Marcus, Ry, and Dan,

This shall address each of you separately, then together.

First, Marcus, I have been hesitant to reveal your email address to anyone for quite a while, due to the sensitive nature of your profession. However, the fact that Geoff Williams chose to offer to reveal it to me, the fact that a recent review from Kirkus Reviews appears indicative of the anonymous reviewer having chosen extreme skepticism of the reality of the most sensitive presentations reported in *Alternative Beginnings and Endings of All Things: Science, Religion, Politics, and Cards, Hypervolume II* (2024), and the general trends of several other things have led to my choosing to perform this forwarding. I am not looking to have the review changed, as that would be like doctoring a documentary film that has already been published without adding some clarification that the doctoring had happened; however, several possibilities of future relations between Kirkus Reviews and me are contingent on how things unfold from here, plus I am testing your email address to see if I might report to you something truly suspicious from the night of February 1, 2022 that I have only previously reported to the CIA. If your electronic mail address bounces, then I will plan to promptly inform Ry and Dan of that bouncing, such that they can accurately perceive the context in a way constructive toward benefiting the future of the lives of sentient beings in general. Also, if your email address bounces, then I probably will not wind up reporting to the FBI the aforementioned suspicious February 1, 2022 item referenced above. Furthermore, if the email does not bounce, then you will only have a brief window of opportunity to notify me not to include Ry and Dan in my process of informing you, and via you the FBI, about portions of conversations from that evening of the thirty-second day of Twenty-Twenty-Two.

I believe it completely justified for me to perform this set of communication, and, whether or not the FBI or the entire federal government were to wind up considering it to be fully justified, I expect to have no regrets about it, because it is part of what the best of my ability to discern the proper times, seasons, purposes, spaces, and everything and everyone else to coordinate into being at this instant of performing it.

Second, Ry, there have been several patterns that I noticed over time that have contributed to why I am performing this forwarding.

Third, Dan, whichever way this happens to proceed, thank you for your role in facilitating how Kirkus Reviews has reviewed several of my books.

Fourth, addressing all three of you together, happy holidays in terms of whichever holidays that you currently find the most appropriate to your situations!

Maurice James Blair

From: Jim Blair <████████████████>
Sent: Wednesday, September 15, 2021 1:20 PM
To: Marcus Padow <██████@fbi.gov>
Subject: Re: [EXTERNAL EMAIL] - _____, , or regarding "Form 3X" or "not Form 3X"

Marcus,

That is fine. In early September I learned directly from the FEC about my options on potential next steps regarding this matter.

By the way, I purchased *Doctor Who: Lost in Time _ Collection of Rare Episodes* {BBC Video 3-disc DVD video} about 10 3/4 or 10 2/3 years ago, more or less or thereabouts. I enjoyed examining that many years ago and occasionally revisiting portions thereof.

Hope all is well with you,
Jim

P.S. When unidentified men robbed my mother and ransacked our apartment on 9/22/2015, she at that time told me (and presumably) HPD that it involved multiple Black men with an unusual accent and speaking quickly. However, on April 8th, 2021 or thereabouts she believed that she remembered clearly that it involved two Black men and three Hispanic men, and that they wore white gloves that extended more than halfway up the forearms. (She did not clarify if the Hispanics were Black Hispanics, White Hispanics, Asian Hispanics, Very-Mixed-Race Hispanics, etc.) On April 9th, 2021 I ... spoke with some people. On April 10th, 2021 I spoke with HPD regarding multiple matters. Just FYI.

From: Marcus Padow <██████@fbi.gov>
Sent: Tuesday, September 7, 2021 3:45 PM
To: Jim Blair <████████████████>
Subject: RE: [EXTERNAL EMAIL] - _____, , or regarding "Form 3X" or "not Form 3X"

Hi Jim,

Thank you for Bcc: me on your last email. I am over in Miami right now and do not work on this topic, so I have neither subject matter knowledge or regional expertise on the issues discussed in your email. With that said, I was not able to identify anything in the information you provided that would seem to meet the threshold associated with the matter being a potential federal crime.

If you believe that what you heard or observed is a federal violation, I would recommend that you either use the FBI general tip line (https://www.fbi.gov/contact-us) or reach out directly to the FBI Houston Field Office (https://www.fbi.gov/contact-us/field-offices/houston), since this office covers the region where I am guessing, based on your email, the alleged violation took place.

Hope all is well with you,
Marcus

From: Jim Blair <████████████████>
Sent: Tuesday, August 31, 2021 1:03 PM
To: oig@fec.gov; info@fec.gov
Cc: CommissionerLee@sec.gov; newstips@abc13.com; FOX26HoustonNews@foxtv.com; Carol Wang <carolwang@cmcdllc.com>; Maurice Blair <███████████████>; ███████████████;

Subject: [EXTERNAL EMAIL] - _____, , or regarding "Form 3X" or "not Form 3X"

Dear Federal Election Commission:

Here is a transcript of select excerpts from an August 19th, 2021 e-mail I sent to two organizations:

_____

"Sometime circa September-to-November 2018, Thomas Sartor and several other men then-employed by The Financial Advisory Group"

...

"in Houston"

...

...

"'hereafter referred to as "FinGroup"'"

...

", including yours truly, were speaking with each other at a lunch gathering or something similar. Sartor expressed that he felt troubled about his alleged knowledge that Steve Estrin (also then of FinGroup) had been providing a place to stay for a Democratic Party campaign person (who was not otherwise of his household) rent-free."

...

"He said he was troubled because he thought it was potentially tantamount to an unreported in-kind political contribution.

I do not know for sure whether Thomas Sartor spoke of fully accurate knowledge of something that actually happened, though based on knowing him fairly well, I believe him to have very likely been speaking accurately regarding that."

_____

_____

_____

Here are names and e-mail addresses of two persons who may or may not be persons of interest (and who I believe would very likely be helpful to include in your investigation, whether they attempt to give you misleading answers or correctly-leading answers... if you choose to investigate):

██(From here, I estimate about a 50% chance that he has had direct contact with Steve Estrin.)
███████████████████████████████████(From here, I estimate about an 85% chance that he has had direct contact with Steve Estrin.)

...

Regards,

Maurice James Blair

[39]

"Fw: Attn: SEC & Attn: Michael C. Kelsheimer" or "forward: an act of skewering and disclosing" or "
_____ _____ "

From: Maurice Blair ██████████████
Sent: Tuesday, August 31, 2021 10:59 AM
To: Maurice Blair ██████████████
Subject: Fw: Attn: SEC & Attn: Michael C. Kelsheimer

██
██

----- Forwarded Message -----
From: Maurice Blair ██████████████
To: CommissionerLee@sec.gov <commissionerlee@sec.gov>; CommissionerPeirce@sec.gov
<commissionerpeirce@sec.gov>; CommissionerRoisman@sec.gov <commissionerroisman@sec.gov>;
CommissionerCrenshaw@sec.gov <commissionercrenshaw@sec.gov>; MKelsheimer@grayreed.com
<mkelsheimer@grayreed.com>
Sent: Tuesday, August 10, 2021, 06:34:26 PM CDT
Subject: Attn: SEC & Attn: Michael C. Kelsheimer

Dear Securities and Exchange Commission and Mr. Kelsheimer:

On account of how The Financial Advisory Group committed libel against me in portions of the cease and desist demand that I received earlier today, and on account of evaluating all factors to the best of my ability, I believe it best to inform you of the following.

Although a) The Financial Advisory Group (located in Houston, TX; in most instances hereafter, "FinGroup") in its termination letter left a blank space as the reason for termination and b) FinGroup personnel only spoke in terms of "It was an executive decision" and the equivalently vague "Things just didn't work out" at the exit interview, I believe an incident from circa September to October 2018 was likely a factor.

Yes, Michael Berry and I discussed multiple incidents involving FinGroup during portions of his August 6th, 2021 morning show. However, here is one of the things I withheld from that conversation.

Around September or October 2018, Natasha McDaniel, Chris Kolenda, and I had a conversation. [I do not recall with certainty whether or not there was a fourth person present.] Natasha mentioned something that allegedly happened behind the scenes at Tesla. As a relatively new employee, and with a spirit of goodwill, I asked if it might be something we should bring to the attention of Juan, for procedures to protect against the risk of insider trading. Natasha reacted with condemnation toward my even daring to speak of this out loud. Also, she showed signs of suddenly considering my reputation to have died there and then in her eyes in connection with this conversation. At one point she said with extreme hostility something like, "At some point you know just where you stand with some people."

Natasha spoke of alleged knowledge of details regarding some internal communications between Tesla employees, although I do not remember for certain exactly what she said transpired in those communications.

At some point I spoke with Juan about it, and he indicated that it would fall into the category of being nonpublic-though-immaterial information with respect to the capital markets. For a long time I had confidence in FinGroup CCO Juan Martinez's judgment about that incident and considered it have simply been an unfortunate choice.

However, as events led to multiple revelations on July 19th, 2021, I came to much more thoroughly question Juan Martinez's motives and judgment. On that day, I decided that, to the best of my judgment, the three people who treated me most unethically in my life were Natasha McDaniel [of FinGroup], the man who molested me briefly on an outdoor bench in Taiwan when I was a very young child, and Juan Martinez [of FinGroup]. That soon led me to contemplate communicating with the SEC about the circa September to October 2018 incident in case it would be helpful for the SEC to know about it, and that soon led me to contemplate communicating with the SEC about my general impression of CCO Juan Martinez's ethics. However, I repeatedly dismissed the idea of telling this to the SEC until today.

...

For clarification about the reference to FinGroup committing libel against me I present a list:

0) Here is an excerpt from the letter: "You have trespassed at company facilities to stalk employees, harassed employees via social media, unwanted calls, and, most recently, you have inappropriately included The Financial Advisory Group employees in communications with various chess organizations."
1) In contrast with the allegation of trespassing at company facilities, the reality is that I have completely avoided the building at 5599 San Felipe St, Houston, TX since my termination from FinGroup, although I have briefly visited the parking lot about five times.
2) When I visited that parking lot, the purpose was not to stalk employees; indeed I had no expectation of meeting employees those times, especially on account of how each visit ranged from approximately under one minute to approximately five minutes. The purpose of my visiting the parking lot was religious in nature.
3) Regarding the social media, calls, and the cc'ing FinGroup employees on e-mails to chess organizations, I believe I was fully justified in exercising my First Amendment right in those cases, especially given the behavior of multiple FinGroup personnel toward me. Those communications were helpful in the process of my healing from the harm that multiple FinGroup personnel did to me and to evaluate things like if and when to decide to contact the SEC. Also, whether the SEC personnel will choose to believe this e-mail to be appropriate for SEC purposes or not, there is no way for me to tell for sure at the time of composing and sending it. However, considering the totality of my interactions with FinGroup personnel plus all other factors to the best of my ability, I truly believe it most likely more helpful to the SEC for me to send this than to refrain from sending it.

Regards,

Maurice James Blair

Chapter Three: An Interzonal Featuring Cobalt, Thorium, and Strontium

An Introduction to This Intermediate Zone: The "Deep Thoughts by Jack Handey" segments of *Saturday Night Live* were hilarious to me back when I watched some of them in the early 1990s, yet only on rare occasions in the 21st century have I chosen to revisit any of them.

"Here's a Deep Thought or Ten Thousand" by M. James Blair

In 1991 I started using a Donnay Cobalt tennis racket. Although I have probably played less tennis in the period of October 1992 to December 2024 than I had usually played monthly in the January-1991-to-May-1991 and September-1991-to-June-1992 periods, that Cobalt tennis racket was still among my possessions the most recent time I checked for it.

During much of the early 2010 to September 2015 period I routinely drove a Chevrolet Cobalt at least twice per week, sometimes twelve or more times spread over seven days per week. Sometimes I wonder why when I was about 10-16 years old and my father would go on at length about comparative nuclear weaponry he would mainly talk about the nuclear fallout from Strontium-90, without bringing up discussion about the nuclear fallout from Cobalt-60. I mean, for goodness' sake and for mass extinctions' sake, I found out in 1997 or thereabouts that Kubrick's *Dr. Strangelove* (1964) emphasizes deadly fallout from Cobalt and Thorium, and in the 2000s I noticed that Abrahams and Post's *Beneath the Planet of the Apes* (1970) emphasizes megafallout from Cobalt. Why did my father emphasize Strontium-90 so much, whereas Stanley Kubrick emphasized some combo of Cobalt and Thorium isotopes and Mort Abrahams and Ted Post emphasized some ultra-lethal mega-unleashing of Cobalt-60 and other radioactive isotopes? On another note, at least one bonus feature of the aforementioned 1970 motion picture film included someone who participated in the project saying that although it made good money at the box office, none of the people involved with making it felt very good about its ending. In contrast, to me the risk of human extinction and the ethics of scenarios of human extinction vs. scenarios of human survival are very lovable!!!

Long before I consciously found out that the movies *Dr. Strangelove* and *Beneath the Planet of the Apes* even existed, a combination of my father and various cultural artifacts had already acclimated me to a thorough acceptance that the human race will probably almost definitely become totally extinct someday, one way or another. Whether it's human extinction by the supernatural, human extinction by the natural, or by anything else, the regular planes and volumes of reality will probably sooner or later become devoid of human beings in this universe, with humans going into the great beyond to face some type of judgment day as per very religious notions, with humans going by the time of the death of the universe or earlier in accordance with a prevailing astrophysics set of notions, or by some hybrid of the two.

Therefore, two questions: 1) Why did they choose such different preferences of which lethal radioactive long-half-life isotopes (Cobalt-60, General Set of Thorium Isotopes, Strontium-90, &c.) to emphasize to whom? 2) Why do we not find a way to increase the amount of public discourse about the ethics of human extinction versus the ethics of human survival and the related issues of every extinction versus every survival and such, with an acceptance that there can be many meanings of many lives and deaths?

CHAPTER FOUR:

More Screenshots and Similar Items

Date: Wed, 03 Aug 2011 11:01:44 AM CDT
From: "Maurice J. Blair" <███████████>
To: <██████████@█.fbi.gov>
Subject: greetings, fellow Duke Alumnus

Marcus,

This is Jim Blair AKA Maurice AKA Hoser. Geoff Williams was kind enough to let me know how to reach you. Congratulations on finding a special career role!

If you don't mind my asking, did you get a chance to see Transformers: Dark of the Moon?

I missed the previous Transformers movies, though I watched some of the TV series when I was a kid, then I decided to watch this year's film installment. I really enjoyed it, especially since it seems to do for the space programs and geopolitics of 1961 to 2011 what Homer did for some of the warfare and political history involving Ancient Greece.

BTW, I don't know anything about D.B. Cooper other than publicly available information; however, imagining things related to his story in a style similar to some episodes of The Twilight Zone led to my development of a 2005 short story I wrote in April of that year and entered into the 74th annual version of a writing contest. I didn't officially win any awards from the contest, btw, lol ;-)

If you have any topics you'd like to discuss with me by e-mail or telephone, just let me know.

It's great to be back in contact with you after all these years!

YITB,

Jim Blair

<u>Part One of a Lightly-Redacted Transcript of an October 1, 2011 Message From Maurice J. Blair to Katherine Navarette, including Copies of an Earlier Message from Katherine to Maurice and an Even Earlier Message From Maurice to Katherine</u>

Kathy,

Just about twenty or thirty minutes before this e-mail I watched "Alejandro" for the first time and enjoyed it. The video was quite surreal with its visual stylings.

Soon after that, I watched "November Rain" for the first time in years. I enjoyed it and it reminded me of multiple bizarre things from my past involving multiple people. It probably has that effect on many people when they haven't seen the video in years and they view it again.

Some time when I set aside enough minutes, I plan to watch "Telephone," Enrique Iglesias' "I Like It," Fat Boy Slim's "Weapon of Choice," Beyonce's "Sweet Dreams," and Madonna's "Bad Girl," under the plan we discussed earlier this year. I know I've been kind of slow with viewing some music videos you're interested in, but at least it's some progress with watching one more Lady Gaga video today and watching that special power ballad G&R video again for the first time since many years ago.

With *Atlas Shrugged*, I read just a very brief excerpt last year, mainly part of the introduction in a version with Amazon.com's "Look Inside feature." With *The Fountainhead*, I read up to something like page 43 in an edition I checked out from Houston Public Library last year. These seemed interesting, and maybe someday I'll read more from Ayn Rand. Some of what she says really makes sense within some context and to some degree, though not in other contexts and not to other degrees. In some ways that can be said of all idea structures, as one of the manifestations of what Buddhists call "the emptiness of all things." Taoists may attribute some of this to the Tao.

With Tarot, there are many ways that people can define "readings." For me, the main thing about Tarot involves the super-powerful extra capabilities of psychological insight and insight beyond psychological insight and related tools. Some of this may be called readings or something else. Take a look at http://www.sacred-texts.com/tarot/sot/index.htm when you get a chance, and you may get a glimpse of some of what Tarot can do outside of pop culture preconceptions of it.

I might someday join Netflix, but if I do, then it would probably be after I get my career on more solid footing. My employer currently has me working part-time part of the year and full-time part of the year.

Also, I enjoy TV and movies, yet in recent years a large part of my TV viewing tends to lean toward a mixture of news and sports.

My father and I enjoyed watching *2001* on the big screen very much. Later in the summer, my parents and I enjoyed watching *Xanadu* on a big screen at another outdoor-venue free event in Houston.

Spread out over many months, I've been in the early stages of learning the basics of how to play the game of bridge. What do you think about bridge?

Maurice

------ Original Message ------
Received: Sat, 24 Sep 2011 11:03:39 AM CDT
From: Katherine Navarrete
To: "Maurice J. Blair"
Subject: Re: hope & hegemonies

Hi Maurice,

Fair warning, this is just a jumble of thoughts, not composed in any coherent way. A coherent email would take another 2 years.

How did your video viewings go? An outdoor experience of *2001* sounds especially cool...in face any full screen experience of that movie sounds great. I've only seen it on a TV. :/

Did you ever make the plunge and sign up for Netflix? Winter is a great time to do it...though I guess it doesn't get as cold in TX as it does up here, less impulse to hibernate, probably. I love chatting about all the TV shows I watch on Netflix...though you seem more of a movie guy, if I am not mistaken.

Have you read *Atlas Shrugged*? I never have, therefore did not watch the movie. I really liked *The Fountainhead* when I read it in high school, though the rape scene really got me angry. I think if I re-read it now, I wouldn't like it so much anymore, and that I would find Ayn Rand vain and egotistical and annoying. How did you like the book?

Following the article you linked to a while back, do you read Tarot cards/get readings?

Not much to report from my end. I just got back from a few weekends away, and Christophe is out of town this weekend, as is my best friend (but not together) so I sort of have the weekend to myself. Catching up on emails, mail, tasks around the house, etc seems a fine way to spend it.

Hope you are well.

--Kathy

On Wed, Jun 29, 2011 at 2:10 PM, Maurice J. Blair wrote:

> Kathy,
>
> Happy Belated Birthday!
>
> If you don't mind my asking, exactly which day in June is your birthday?
>
> I hope that when I get around to viewing more music videos my comments will
> prove interesting and useful for you. As a little prelude, I'll mention
> that a
> very long time ago I saw the video for "November Rain," and even before you
> mentioned it in an e-mail to me, I'd already purchased a download of it
> from
> iTunes. Although I haven't seen the video for it in years, I very much look
> forward to viewing it again, when I feel the time is right.
>
> Something that may inspire diverse reactions among people when they find
> out
> about it is that I currently have a three-DVD set checked out from Houston
> Public Library. It has the 1956 movie version of *The Ten Commandments*, the
> 1923 version, plus some bonus features. On a related note, my father and I
> plan to experience *2001: A Space Odyssey* on the big screen on Friday at
> Miller
> Outdoor Theatre in Houston.
>

of a Lightly-Redacted Transcript of an October 1, 2011 Message (This part
continues and concludes a copy of a June 29, 2011 Message That Had Been Included on
Display as a Prior Round that led to the October 2011 Message)

> If you want to discuss anything with me before or after when I watch and
> share
> commentary on the additional music videos you recently suggested, please
> feel
> free to select a topic... or multiple topics.
>
>
> Kind Regards,
>
> Maurice
>
>

January 7, 2025 Comments on that set of 29 JUN to 01 OCT 2011 electronic communications:
Both Kathy and I had left several normally-italicized titles unitalicized prior to the redaction
process for the copy here. The referenced 8:15 P.M. CDT, Saturday, July 30, 2011
JULYDOSCOPE screening of *Xanadu* (1980) at Discovery Green happened while the main
political leader of Houston, Texas was Mayor Annise Parker. The percentage of all the mayors
of major U.S. cities during each period from 1981 onward who would have dared to consider
it a good idea to provide a free public screening downtown of that 1980 film is probably
microscopic. Nevertheless, the powers that be that ran Houston as of 2011 made it happen
anyway!

Here is something related that I have told few people before: When I checked out a home
video recording of *Grease* (1978) from a library in the second quarter of 2011, I hit pause
during part of the opening animation and suddenly discovered that there on the screen, plain
as day, was a swastika!! Bear in mind that the opening animation for that film also includes
a reference to the film *The Ten Commandments* (1956). Additionally, bear in mind how the
other generally-critically-acclaimed movie *The Ten Commandments* (1923) has quite a
hierarchical and standards-based approach to arriving at transcendental effectiveness,
whereas the generally-critically-panned movie *Xanadu* (1980) has quite an egalitarian and
extreme-flexibility-based approach to arriving at transcendental effectiveness. To bring this
all back home, there seems a parallel between the aforementioned surprising freeze frame
discovery in the playback of a disc of *Grease* and how a scene early in *Xanadu* includes the
idea of an entire being's physical presence mysteriously appearing in a frame unexpectedly.

Science, Religion, Politics, and Cards, pp. 190-191 includes a copy of a follow-up message
from me to Kathy, reporting to her some of the aftermath of getting around to watching
referenced music videos years later.

The next page features a redacted screenshot of the earliest part of that thread.

Date: Wed, 29 Jun 2011 01:10:06 PM CDT
From: "Maurice J. Blair" < ██████████ >
To: "Katherine Navarrete" < ██████████████ >
Subject: hope & hegemonies

[More Details] [Print Preview]

Kathy,

Happy Belated Birthday!

If you don't mind my asking, exactly which day in June is your birthday?

I hope that when I get around to viewing more music videos my comments will prove interesting and useful for you. As a little prelude, I'll mention that a very long time ago I saw the video for "November Rain," and even before you mentioned it in an e-mail to me, I'd already purchased a download of it from iTunes. Although I haven't seen the video for it in years, I very much look forward to viewing it again, when I feel the time is right.

Something that may inspire diverse reactions among people when they find out about it is that I currently have a three-DVD set checked out from Houston Public Library. It has the 1956 movie version of The Ten Commandments, the 1923 version, plus some bonus features. On a related note, my father and I plan to experience 2001: A Space Odyssey on the big screen on Friday at Miller Outdoor Theatre in Houston.

If you want to discuss anything with me before or after when I watch and share commentary on the additional music videos you recently suggested, please feel free to select a topic... or multiple topics.

Kind Regards,

Maurice

_____

[48]

Cassie,

As a first step toward a tennis practice, I suggest that you help with identifying locations that could work well for you.

Would either Bayland Park (6400 Bissonnet, just west of Hillcroft) or the Memorial Park Tennis Center be practical locations for you?

Or do you have a more convenient location to suggest?

Once I receive your response, I can verify the days and times of near-term availability of the location and my schedule, then call you to discuss your availability to schedule and the next steps of arranging to make the practice happen.

Kind Regards,

Maurice

A January 7, 2025 Note Regarding That: Dental Hygienist Cassie Dullea, whom I met via a Meetup event in which she and I were in the same group, informed me upon first meeting me approximately in May or June of 2011 that she enjoyed tennis. I played on the Hanks High School Varsity Tennis Team part of the time from January 1991 to about August 1992.

She declined to ever directly respond to that e-mail message from me to her. However, she and I became Facebook friends for quite a number of years, until for some reason(s) unbeknownst to me (and I have considered several hypotheses on a few occasions), she unfriended me in March 2021. The post of which a copy appears on the next page was something with which I chose to memorialize the beginning and the end of the friendship between her and me.

A lightly redacted copy of what I posted soon after noticing Cassie Dullea had unfriended me:

Farewell to a Facebook Friendship (Version 2021.03.23)

March 23, 2021

Just a few minutes ago, one of "my" "then-Facebook" "friends" evidently "unfriended" "me" on "Facebook." I will decline to name her here in this post, though I remember her name. She and I were never more than just friends, and I never made an attempt to in any way bring up the idea of being any thing more than friends. Yes, I invited her to play tennis once some time around 2011, she politely avoided the tennis practice, and at some stage she and I became Facebook friends. (This is a friends-only post, though I believe it very likely for some friends to forward it to other persons. Be forewarned, though, any alterations from the original are such that I would expect perhaps eighteen-raised-to-twenty-third-factorial of a known-or-unknown spiritual channeling of some ancient text or texts or context or contexts!!) Just prior to the apparent/evidential unfriending, she had posted a photograph of the Max I. Dimont book _Jews,_God_and_History_ appearing to have a Calvin & Hobbes comic sticking partway out as a kind of bookmark. The Calvin & Hobbes (or similar) comic seemed to have a child saying something like, "Look, mom just got me a new head outfit." The entity other than the child had a response that only partially displayed, and part of it I remember as displaying "Not look..." Someone else responded to her with a list of some Internet prophecies from a while ago, (I decline to state here the origin or possible origins or URL of the reference from that someone else.) I responded to that someone else's response, stating something like, "'I would think ... (or shall I say "hypothesize") that the most extreme "vaccination" threat could be if a government were to implement a mandatory brain-chip implantation, at first appearing to be nonthreatening, then transitioning into an ("Orwellian"-sty.le) Big Bro(ther) government control mechanism... {continuation to be determined or not to be determined}.'"

2 comments

Maurice James Blair
Ah, but it could be ambiguous as to whether the invitation to play tennis was in some way an insinuation of a beyond-friendship intent or not an insinuation of a beyond-friendship intent. Either way, I will add here that ... (see next response below)

3y   Like   Reply

Maurice James Blair
... I added on that evidently-former-friend's Facebook (profile / list of posts/etc.) a note that it was only a few minutes after to the best of my memory I had first clearly cognized that the name "MAX I. DIMONT" existed.

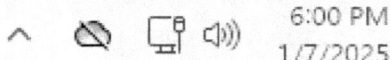

6:00 PM
1/7/2025

<u>A January 7, 2025 Follow-up Comment:</u> Please note that many have considered via 20th century and early 21st century science fiction and engineering and nonfiction science the threat of totalitarian use of brain chips. When I brought it up on her FB page, my idea was to point toward a future risk that a government could tell its citizens that the only proper immunization against something would be for their brains to receive a computer chip implant.

Keil,

Please forward this to the appropriate person, if you can.

There was an article some time in the past few years, though I don't recall who the publisher was, and in it was an idea involving possible future Olympics baseball. The author suggested that since the Summer Olympics have previously had scheduling difficulties with extra-inning baseball games and will not be having baseball in the 2012 games, they might consider modifying the extra-innings format (for their purposes) if they someday bring baseball back. Specifically, the idea involved a baserunner automatically going to first base to begin each side's half of each necessary extra inning to speed things up. I don't recall if there was another nuance to the suggestion.

Here are two ideas I've thought about, though there are probably others who have thought of them:

1) To have each extra inning from the eleventh onward in future Olympics be "mini-innings" in which the first runner automatically goes to third (not attributable to any human pitcher in the box score; rather, to "Mini-Inning 3B Allowance" or something similar) and each team only gets one out. [A pitcher who pitched three mini-innings in a row would have one inning counted toward the box score and not be charged for any runners scoring from third; they would be charged to a nonroster phantom pitcher called "mini-inning 3B allowance" or something similar.] [or there could be a different approach to the box score and statistics.]

2) To have a maximum of twelve "normal innings" of plate appearances for the designated visiting team and only eleven for the designated home team in future Olympics. Basically, if the score is tied at the ends of the ninth, tenth, and eleventh innings, the top of the twelfth has up to three outs and begins with noone on base, yet there is a kind of sudden-death feature: If the visiting team fails to score, the designated home team wins by a declared bonus run. If the visiting team scores, then the designated visiting team immediately wins. [I'll leave it open to others to initiate ideas about how the bonus run and other special 12th inning details should be accounted for in the box score, if anyone chooses to conjecture on this.]

BTW, I haven't set out to do research on what ideas are already floating out there regarding these issues that might affect the 2016 summer games and later olympiads, and, as far as I know, noone else has presented these two ideas to me.

Sincerely,

Maurice J. Blair

correcting part of your record (regarding TX 9-443-558)

Maurice Blair <... ✉ Wed, Dec 11, 2024, 2:51 PM ☆ 😊 ↩ ⋮

to copyinfo, Steve ▾

Dear Copyright Office Personnel,

Although it is not at the level at which a court of law would consider it something worthy of suing the U.S. Copyright Office for defamation of character over, nevertheless, in terms of some deep levels of reality it is at least a small bearing of false witness against me that your office took the stance earlier today of judging it to the position of the space between 1 and 9 being my error and not the copyright office's error, before taking additional steps. That involves how, at about 1:30 PM EST [12:30 PM CST] 11 December 2024, Kingsleigh Kipling of your team spoke to me over the phone a combination of stating that a record he viewed within your office's system led him to believe such, and he then told me that your office officially takes that position; however, as you shall probably be able to see from the pdf copy included here, the paper that I sent into the mail to you had "1976" completely together without any spaces.

(Reference: part of 2a on page 1 of the attached pdf, which includes one accurate digital copy each for two different applications.)

Yes, there could be some third alternative, yet that would nearly defy the imagination. I sent in the exact same application that my Brother Printer/Scanner scanned such as to match what I witnessed in physical print as having shown "1976" all together, without the space.

Mr. Kingsleigh Kipling did prove helpful in several ways, and he indicated having forwarded my concern for the typo and having arranged the probable start of the correction process, yet he imposed upon me the idea that "it doesn't matter" that the typo exists and makes part of the online record fragment the listing of me as an author such as to appear as one with a birth year "1976" and another with a birth year "1 976." I mentioned to him that even though for something like a court of law it might not matter, with the sorts of experiences that I have had in recent years, for anyone to nit-pick anything could make an impact, and that includes whatever public records there would be.

If he had told me, "What I see of our records at the office makes it appear to be your error, though I do not know if something got doctored, whether by scanning equipment slipping or whatever else. Let's not worry about labeling blame of who or what is at fault. Let's focus on fixing this," then I would not be resorting to sending you this sharply critical message and cc'ing my estate planning attorney (who is not currently on a billable time with me for any issues though still open to occasional interpersonal communications, and whom I might consider hiring again someday for something or another).

However, what that Mr. Kipling actually said to me was nearly identical to, "What I see in our records shows that you had the space between the 1 and the 9. I am not going to argue this with you further. It is the copyright office's position that it was your error. Period. End of story."

That is the sort of thing that at this stage in my life, no matter who does it (any age, gender, rank, social status, financial status, race, religion, species, realm of existence, or anything else), I will go full tilt "Nemo me impune lacessit" on the person or other type of being, with whether I live or die and whether the human race goes extinct or not in any given instant of time being immaterial to me compared to the great value of favoring the bearing of true witness over the bearing of false witness. Especially in service to the enlightenment of sentient beings.

Johnny Cash (1932-2003) was quoted long ago as saying, "My arms are too short to box with God." However, J.R.R. Tolkien (1892-1973), Yeshe Tsogyal (c. 767-817), and others have shown that sometimes Reality forces beings to fight against impostors to divine authority, such that whoever or whatever might in some context seem to be God and yet be devoid of actual full legitimacy each being should on at least some occasions consider to have adequate means with which to fight against.

Yes, your office can take that sort of false position on this, but, yes, also, I can present to you (and, if and when I might ever choose to do so at any stage in the future when the time, season, and purpose to align for it to be or to seem to be correct for it, to the general public, via copying this very e-mail message's main text to some future post and/or publication, though probably redacting my signature from the application copy attachment in order to protect myself against excessive risks) a set of true witness refutation of the phraseology and conceptualization that he stated to me over the phone.
   This is a way that the record can be clear such as to not give those who at times have shown such unbelievable hostility (and failure of understanding) toward me that much more ammunition with which to go flying off (a ledge or a cliff or whatever) into excessive hostility.

I did not give any specific examples to Kingsleigh Kipling on this, instead speaking with brief abstractions, but many such examples are contained in the very book at the center of this anomaly issue (i.e., the one with TX 9-443-558 as its registration number).
   Many additional examples can found elsewhere in this world, including how one of the former business associates, a person whom I mentioned in that book in connection with the nickname Bill Walker, instructed me in either 2014 or 2015 with saying something very much like, "You've gotta think about this sort of report we're putting together from the perspective of if lawyers look at it in court and are ready to say things like, 'Look at this here: The numbers do not foot properly, because they were lazy and did not fix a one dollar error. If we cannot trust them to have their act together enough to avoid a one dollar error there, then how much more should we call into question everything about their competence as an accounting firm in putting together review reports?' Imagine that, later on, people take this to a court case and both sides look for any little thing that they can latch onto to manipulate the jury in favor of their side and against the other side."

Yes, after he was no longer among my associates, a fellow named Marc Schlesinger came along and presented me in early 2016 or thereabouts with the opposite idea regarding the very same type of report, saying something like, "One dollar? It's so small it doesn't matter much. Here's a dollar. [Demonstrating the pulling out of one dollar from his wallet.] I could just hand you a dollar to take care of a one-dollar difference in the numbers."

However, time has proven that there are people all over the place who tend to latch onto anything, including how it seems plausible that some could look up an online records search, see both "Blair, Maurice James, 1976" and "Blair, Maurice James, 1 976" as separate entries and think something like, "Lookey there, I don't have to give a damn whether it was that author's error that led to the separation of entries and the space between 1 and 9 or if it was the copyright office's error or if it was just some computer thing; this is clearly a clue that the fellow has been a fool who rushes in where angels fear to tread and that something to do with that behavioral flaw has led to this paralleling him with the yearling deer in the 1946 film *The Yearling*. I met him before, and he didn't make that great an impression on me back then, and, now, this seems one extra clue from the Internet to regard him as something very much like a one-year-old deer who foolishly goes into areas where it doesn't belong and therefore deserves to be shot dead. He clearly deserves little or no respect, and he could deserve to die at any time by any means such as to be less of a nuisance to people who truly matter, and he is not among the people who truly matter at all."

Of course, that sort of thinking would be flawed in many ways, some of which might become evident to such a person if (s)he might bother to read two or more books of *The Science, Religion, Politics, and Cards Trilogy*, of which *Alternative Beginnings and Endings of All Things* is the middle hypervolume. As some people have mentioned every now and then, likely spread over thousands of years, sometimes things reflect the perspective, "Ignorance is lethal."

Still, I have found it very useful since 2020 to work hard to try not to give people with those sorts of mentalities extra ammunition with which to hate me on false pretenses, except insofar as it sometimes can prove helpful to give them more opportunity to smoke themselves out as deserving rebuke.

That being said, Mr. Kipling did prove helpful in several ways.

After the online submission form would not allow completion due to the "turnstile catchpha" error repeating many times (even with changing to two other browsers in accordance with technical support's advice as given in a separate phone call, after a copyright office woman who identified herself as Ms. Woods had advised me that the online submission form was the right way to proceed at that juncture), he indicated that he communicated to the appropriate parties the request to fix the issue. Also, he informed me that the ███████████████ address is proper in this case, which corrected my previous perception (which had involved an email address that is supposed to be reserved for responding to questions from the copyright office, rather than to be used for this sort of case).

Overall, I consider his role in this to have been helpful, though with room for improvement.

Also, please do not jump to the conclusion of this involving any attempt to rush you on making the change. It should be reasonably timely, but it is not very urgent.

Insofar as the typo remains online, it can prove helpful in luring people in the general public who might deserve to have more consequences of karma land on them wind up with those consequences of that karma landing on them in a timely fashion, via them smoking themselves out to Reality unwittingly since they might not know better. That is, whether or not you or I ever find out in this lifetime about them bringing such combinations of sowing and reaping upon themselves.

That being said, taking a reasonable approach to fixing the issue in the moderately near future could prove helpful--to at least a small degree-to all or nearly all sentient beings.

In case helpful to your technical support, I am also including two examples of screenshots of the "turnstile catchpha" error page that I ended up facing on my monitor something like 25 or 52 times today.

Regards,
Maurice J. Blair

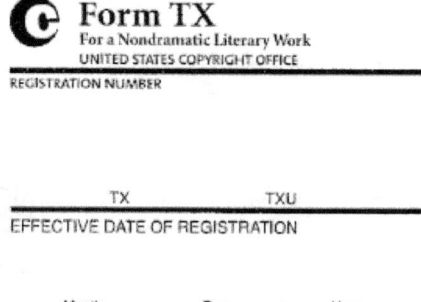

Form TX
For a Nondramatic Literary Work
UNITED STATES COPYRIGHT OFFICE

REGISTRATION NUMBER

TX   TXU
EFFECTIVE DATE OF REGISTRATION

Month   Day   Year

DO NOT WRITE ABOVE THIS LINE. IF YOU NEED MORE SPACE, USE A SEPARATE CONTINUATION SHEET.

TITLE OF THIS WORK ▼
Alternative Beginnings and Endings of All Things: Science, Religion, Politics, and Cards, Hypervolume II

PREVIOUS OR ALTERNATIVE TITLES ▼

PUBLICATION AS A CONTRIBUTION If this work was published as a contribution to a periodical, serial, or collection, give information about the collective work in which the contribution appeared.   Title of Collective Work ▼

If published in a periodical or serial give: Volume ▼   Number ▼   Issue Date ▼   On Pages ▼

NAME OF AUTHOR ▼
Maurice James Blair

DATES OF BIRTH AND DEATH
Year Born ▼   Year Died ▼
1976

Was this contribution to the work a "work made for hire"?
☐ Yes
☑ No

AUTHOR'S NATIONALITY OR DOMICILE
Name of Country
OR { Citizen of United States of America
     { Domiciled in

WAS THIS AUTHOR'S CONTRIBUTION TO THE WORK
Anonymous?   ☐ Yes ☑ No
Pseudonymous? ☐ Yes ☑ No

If the answer to either of these questions is "Yes," see detailed instructions.

NOTE

NATURE OF AUTHORSHIP Briefly describe nature of material created by this author in which copyright is claimed. ▼
All text, artwork, and photographs, except as otherwise specified in the text and de minimis use of public domain materials.

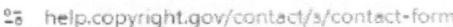

YouTube   Maps

help.copyright.gov says

Turnstile Captcha Failed

Contact Form

Please use the form to contact us. Allow up to ten business days to r

For press/media inquiries, please see Press/Media Information.

Formulario en español

Category:	Other ▾
First Name:	Maurice
Middle Name:	James
Last Name:	Blair
Email:	▇▇▇▇▇▇▇
Phone:	▇▇▇▇▇▇▇
Service Request Number:	Service Request Number (if known)
Title of Work:	Alternative Beginnings and Endings of All Things: Science, Religion, Politics, and Cards, Hyper\
Question:	TX 9-443-558 at this time shows my year of birth as "1 976"--Including a space between the "1" and the "9," whereas my application, dated 8/9/2024 showed "1976". Please fix this.

Submit   Reset

  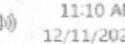 11:10 AM
12/11/2024

[58]

help.copyright.gov says

Turnstile Captcha Failed

Contact Form

Please use the form to contact us. Allow up to ten business days to receive an em

For press/media inquiries, please see Press/Media Information.

Form

Category:	Other
First Name:	Maurice
Middle Name:	James
Last Name:	Blair
Email:	███████████████
Phone:	████████████
Service Request Number:	Service Request Number (if known)
Title of Work:	Alternative Beginnings and Endings of All Things: Science, Religion, Politics, and Cards, Hyperv
Question:	TX 9-443-558 at this time shows my birth year as "1 976" including a space between the "1" an in contrast with how both regular reality and the 8/9/2024 application accord with "1976" dev spaces between digits. Please fix your records.

[59]

Certificate of Registration

This Certificate issued under the seal of the Copyright
Office in accordance with title 17, *United States Code*,
attests that registration has been made for the work
identified below. The information on this certificate has
been made a part of the Copyright Office records.

Shira Perlmutter

United States Register of Copyrights and Director

Registration Number

TX 9-443-558

Effective Date of Registration:
August 12, 2024
Registration Decision Date:
November 12, 2024

Title

Title of Work: Alternative Beginnings and Endings of All Things: Science, Religion, Politics, and Cards, Hypervolume ll

Completion/Publication

Year of Completion: 2024
Date of 1st Publication: May 21, 2024
Nation of 1st Publication: United States

Author

- **Author:** Maurice James Blair
  Author Created: All text, artwork, and photographs, except as otherwise specified in the text and de minimis use of public domain materials.
  Work made for hire: No
  Citizen of: United States
  Year Born: 1976
  Anonymous: No
  Pseudonymous: No

Copyright Claimant

Copyright Claimant: Maurice James Blair
9619 Meadowcroft Dr., Houston, TX, 77063

[60]

Certificate of Registration

This Certificate issued under the seal of the Copyright
Office in accordance with title 17, *United States Code*,
attests that registration has been made for the work
identified below. The information on this certificate has
been made a part of the Copyright Office records.

Shira Perlmutter

United States Register of Copyrights and Director

Registration Number

TX 9-443-558

Effective Date of Registration:
August 12, 2024
Registration Decision Date:
December 17, 2024

Title

Title of Work: Alternative Beginnings and Endings of All Things: Science, Religion, Politics, and Cards, Hypervolume II

Completion/Publication

Year of Completion: 2024
Date of 1st Publication: May 21, 2024
Nation of 1st Publication: United States

Author

- **Author:** Maurice James Blair
  Author Created: All text, artwork, and photographs, except as otherwise specified in the text and de minimis use of public domain materials.
  Work made for hire: No
  Citizen of: United States
  Year Born: 1976
  Anonymous: No
  Pseudonymous: No

Copyright Claimant

Copyright Claimant: Maurice James Blair
9619 Meadowcroft Dr., Houston, TX, 77063

A January 7, 2025 Footnote: Regarding the possibilities of publishers ever using intentional typos as communicative black ops and of publishers' unintentional typos also sometimes serving the minds of beholders with communicative special-forces, psychological-extreme-tactic warfare operations, consider studying pages 129-135 of the very book for which that U.S. Copyright Office registration occurred.

Before moving onward with these discussions, let it be known that when people assume other people to be incapable of major improvements, they could set themselves up for various deathtraps and other traps. Here is a sports analogy: If you consider that someone who has ever had one specific thing happen before that you consider a disqualifier from you having any reason to ever again do anything other than think of that someone with ridicule and disdain, then this could be similar to a person who witnesses a player or team perform poorly during a given week, a given season, or a given combination of seasons, then gives up on the player or team ever again performing well. Imagine a person who gives up on a team that winds up with a winning percentage under 0.300 (i.e., under 30%) during a given sports season, then decides to gamble three-fourths of the person's net worth in a way presuming the other team to not have a prayer in the world of winning a championship within three years. Further, imagine that the team *actually does* win a championship in the second year after the dreadful season, and the person soon goes bankrupt due to the extreme disrespect.

I have noticed many cases of other people making vast improvements to their capabilities in life. Also, I have experienced myself make extraordinary improvements. Many times back when a teenager and many times when in my early 20s I would have been extremely skeptical that anyone could experience as consistently high a feeling of well-being and inner peace the way that I have in recent years. Part of the reason I write is that even though some readers might latch onto one detail here or twenty-five details there and presume me to be what they would consider a highly unsuccessful and highly ineffective person, I know otherwise. Is there room for improvement? Yes, in many respects; however, I have experienced extraordinary improvements in terms of well-being in general. Long-term freedom from dependency on any drugs—whether prescription, over-the-counter, or of another category—is part of this. That was one of the things that the Briana Roth who disrespected me via text messaging communications on May 2, 2024 seemed totally recalcitrant with which to come to grips. Cf. pages 640-669 of *Alternative Beginnings and Endings of All Things*. I had believed that I was plenty clear in my text messaging communications to her and in my supplemental descriptions in that book for many reasonably-intelligent, reasonably well-intentioned people to thoroughly understand beyond what I explicitly stated. However, with the hostile review from Kirkus Reviews, I have come to recognize that it might be best in a book such as this one to clarify a few things. When I mentioned having been very nerdy when I was a teenager yet having eventually grown out of it thoroughly, that was a statement that people could interpret or misinterpret in many ways. As it seems clear that some people have had huge difficulty understanding this, I will clarify part of it further: There are many ways that people think about what makes a person a nerd, a jock, or whatever else; however, when push comes to shove, one thing that virtually everyone respects sooner or later at least some of the time is the sheer ability to conduct all-out warfare with others. Although some ways of interpreting nerdiness could wind up with people thinking of me as being a nerd, when it comes to an all-out fight, I feel absolutely no intimidation from living earthling humans of any rank, any gender, any socioeconomic status, any race, and any religion unless and until they wind up with some ultrabizarre situational threat to my ability to live and die with honor, and, even then, I focus on what I can do to get things to work well.

Even when not popular, I am strong. That has tended to be true, through and through, in terms of how well I dealt with a host of interpersonal interactions from partway into the day of July 12, 2021 onward, systematically overwhelming contemners over and over again in the long run. For example, there was no need to directly attack whomever the anonymous reviewer who provided the review that Kirkus Reviews presented regarding *Alternative Beginnings and Endings of All Things*, because I chose instead to conduct surgical strikes to obliterate many of the demons and delusions, including illusory false gods, that people who would excessively judge that book in those ways might have. Some of that is reflected in what portions of this book—especially some of the remainder from here onward—demonstrate to people. That being said, if someone is so stuck on idea structures of rejecting the very reality of my life itself and the very realities of great ranges of many other people's lives, whether due to bowing down mentally to false absolute mental restrictions of thinking or anything else, then that someone is on track to be rebuked by Reality even as measured by that person's own religion(s) and/or science(s) insofar as true at a deep level of reality, for the sentient being in that case is locking into rejecting huge amounts of reality while oblivious to the fact that the sentient being is doing that. Much of this tends to revolve around using identity groups as a crutch with which to think of oneself as somehow inherently owning a total supremacy over anyone lacking that identity group, which can cause the being who fails to grow out of using that crutch to repeatedly turn a blind eye toward individual spiritual and scientific growth while also turning a blind eye toward the value of respecting those who are outside of that person's list of preferred identity groups yet have, nevertheless, paid their dues in terms of achieving major individual spiritual and scientific growth. Next, here is a general description of how this poison can manifest, in terms of idolatry of / attachment to /excessive-attachment to idea structures: 1) of women as having nearly a total right to be of a higher pecking order position than men, 2) of thinking of Jews as having nearly a total right to be of a higher pecking order position than Buddhists, 3) of thinking of Non-Buddhist Jews as having nearly a total right to be of a higher pecking order position than Buddhist Jews, 4) of thinking of Non-Buddhist Noahidists as having nearly a total right to be of a higher pecking order position than Buddhist Noahidists, 5) of thinking of Black people as having nearly a total right to be of a higher pecking order position than Non-Black people, 6) of thinking of Hispanics as having nearly a total right to be of a higher pecking order position than Non-Hispanics, 7) of thinking of people who consistently and primarily identify religiously as Christians as having nearly a total right to be of a higher pecking order position than people who refrain from consistently and primarily identifying religiously as being Christians, 8) other rigid notions in a vein similar to #1-#7, 9) of men as having nearly a total right to be of a higher pecking order position than women, 10) of thinking of Buddhists as having nearly a total right to be of a higher pecking order position than Jews, 11) of thinking of Buddhist Jews as having nearly a total right to be of a higher pecking order position than Non-Buddhist Jews, 12) of thinking Buddhist Noahidists as having nearly a total right to be of a higher pecking order position than Non-Buddhist Noahidists, 13) of thinking of Non-Black people as having nearly a total right to be of a higher pecking order position than Black people, 14) of thinking of Non-Hispanics as having nearly a total right to be of a higher pecking order position than Hispanics, 15) of thinking of people who refrain from consistently and primarily identifying religiously as being Christians as having nearly a total right to be of a higher pecking order position than people who consistently and primarily identify religiously as Christians, and 16) other rigid notions in a vein similar to #9-#15.

One of the ways that Briana Roth might have otherwise earned more of my respect would have been if she had responded at some stage by texting, "Look, I'm just not feeling right about meeting you again in general. Meanwhile, I do not know you well enough to judge you to clearly be a nerd or of a different category at some deep levels; I'll be agnostic on that. Do I find the way you look, the way you talk, and the way you act to be unattractive in a nerdy way sometimes? Yes. However, I am also aware that different women have different preferences, and I am also aware that some definitions of what makes someone a nerd involve them being at the bottom of social pecking orders. You have on some occasions spoken of having come out on top in psychological warfare battles with various people and organizations. You've witnessed more of your life than I have, and I do not know for sure the full degree of accuracy of your characterizations of yourself and your alleged accomplishments. That being said, it seems perfectly plausible to me that you are indeed very capable of standing up for yourself and others in psychological, interpersonal warfare situations, which would mean that in at least one very important sense, you are not a nerd. Nevertheless, since you have experienced much more of your life than I have, I really don't know for sure just how accurate such a notion might happen to be. Whatever the case may be, I am exhausted by something to do with the entire funky way that you seem to live, act, speak, and write. I'm not interested in meeting you again, and I have grown weary of texting back and forth with you. I already grew tired of phone conversations with you a long time ago. Give me plenty of space by either not bothering me anymore or by spreading out future attempts to contact me. Yes, I am tired of you, but that does not take away from the fact that you may very well have much legitimacy as a human being. Maybe I'll later change my mind. Maybe I'll someday become interested again in interacting with you. I might even feel fine about going back to having phone calls with you and, maybe even meeting you in person again. We might not know what the future holds, but I still choose a basic level of respecting you, even amid the recent conflict. Whether or not this proves to be the last communication we share in this lifetime, best wishes with finding your true spiritual path in the long run, or, if you've already found it, then best wishes with making a good thing better. Ciao!"

However, if you consult an authentic, authorized copy of *Alternative Beginnings and Endings of All Things: Science, Religion, Politics, and Cards, Hypervolume II*, then you may witness that her text reactions were of a very different path than the model of respect outlined above. Therefore, she, having already identified herself as very much a liberal in terms of politics long before the May 2, 2024 text-messaging argument involving coordination, planning, and different ideas of what would constitute respect in that context, added fuel to the fire of conflicts that had escalated from November 21, 2018 onward. That woman, who was evidently a middle-aged adult as of recent years, became one of the many contributors to the pattern of my receiving much more disrespect from 2018-2024 liberals than from 2018-2024 conservatives. As displayed in a screenshot much later in this book, on December 23, 2024, after several other stages of interactions, I sent an e-mail message to one recipient while cc'ing many recipients, including a passage described and transcribed as follows:

-----start of a copy of a passage from the 3:30 P.M. CST Festivus Day 2024 message from M.J.B.-------

At this stage I no longer give a damn about if the Democratic Party goes extinct to be replaced by a suitable replacement liberal party much the way that the Republican Party replaced the Whig Party!!!

If I count up all the disrespect toward the bearing of true witness and all the disrespect by the method of the bearing of false witness, even though the Republican Party has not been all that great, the total vitriol either directly or indirectly aimed at me, my family, my religious affiliations, those outside my affiliations yet clearly railroaded, etc., as indicated by personal experience, news, TV, radio, the Internet, etc.. has the full energy associated with the Democratic Party serving as an affront at several times as much as the Republican Party!!!

Although I cheered for the best in a spirit of agnosticism--whether a Democratic victory in the 2024 general election or a Republican victory in the 2024 general election--recently, in accordance with the plan mentioned in *Alternative Beginnings and Endings of All Things*, and although I recognize *both the Democratic Party and the Republican Party to be dangerous in their own ways*, also as per what I stated in that book, I decided that the best I could tell from all available information, a Republican victory in that would probably be best. I voted that way, it turned out that way, and I have no regret about it.

To help anyone seeing this understand, here is a simple analogy: You are on a team that has to make one move per round, and you get to vote for what move your team will make. The team could be analogous to the human race, America, all sentient beings, etc. Therefore, you vote for what you perceive to be best, yet not every single time you vote do you feel anywhere near entirely sure. If you feel uncertain, then you could cheer for the best choice while logically agnostic toward whether your specific vote is on the best side. When I voted I felt quite unsure. Now, the uncertainty is much smaller. I still have a trace of agnosticism toward this, but just in the past few days I have moved very much toward the right, and your choice to write to me in the manner in which you did is the straw that broke the camel-that-held-the-levee-together's back. The levee has broken.

Now, it is also possible that it might be best for *both the Republican Party and the Democratic Party to go away and get replaced by a new pair of parties*. I do not rule that out in the long run.

I care about soteriology, which I believe a properly functioning First Amendment and a reasonably-liberty-filled U.S. can help very much, yet there are reasons for a degree of skepticism toward both major political parties. That being said, the Republican Party has given my family personally much more reason for confidence than has the Democratic Party. I respect that someone with a very different set of life experiences could think and feel exactly the opposite way. I also covered this in *Alternative Beginnings and Endings of All Things*.

----------end of a copy of a passage from the 3:30 P.M. Festivus Day 2024 message M.J.B. sent---------

Records and commentary on a more complete context for that passage occupies some later portions of this book.

*   *   *   *   *

Imagine team contests with eight team members on each team. Next, imagine team contests with sixteen team members on each team. Pivot now to imagining team contests with forty team members per team.

Do what you choose to do about how to relate, how to refrain from relating, and/or how to transcend the dichotomy of relating-vs.-not-relating everything that has happened up to this juncture of this book with the following artwork diagram:

*   *   *   *   *

Revisit now the ancient idea that it can do something extraordinary for a person's soul to let go of hatred and to choose love, especially a foundation of impersonal spiritual love, toward other sentient beings.

*   *   *   *   *

On December 25, 2024, I sent a message to Dan Nolan of Kirkus Reviews, Marcus Padow of the FBI, and many other recipients. Here is a transcript for the main body of that message:

To Whom It May Concern,

Technical correction regarding the vehicle crash: Memory cleared up enough that I remember now that the wisecrack and the ensuing rebuke were upon first contact between the Chi Delta Chapter of Psi Upsilon-affiliated people with the people who stepped out of the other vehicle, which occurred a while prior to when the police showed up.

Regards,

Maurice James Blair

Fwd: Re: Universal Family Watch

Maurice Blair <████████████████>   Mon, Dec 23, 2024 at 5:47 AM
To: Yin-Hsuan Chiu <██████████████.tw>
Cc: Liza Darnton <████████████████>, Tad Schmaltz <tschmalt@umich.edu>, Dan Nolan <████████.com>, Ry Pickard <██████████.com>, Alex Tse <██████████████.au>, Ming Blair <████████████████>

Sherry,

Several times in recent years, my mother possibly either accurately portrayed something that you had evidently said to her or distorted something that you had evidently said to her. The next message, if all goes smoothly, shall include that. Although you might be uncomfortable with some elements of how I am conducting this set of communication, I believe that it will most likely prove helpful to each person directly affected by it in the medium-to-long run.

Regards,
Jim

---------- Forwarded message ---------
From: **Maurice J. Blair** <██████████████>
Date: Mon, Dec 23, 2024 at 5:41 AM
Subject: Fwd: Re: Universal Family Watch
To: Yin-Hsuan Chiu <██████████████>
Cc: <████████████████>

Sherry,

Another address for me is the ████████████████ address. If your address from many years ago does not bounce, then you shall probably soon be part of a multiparty communication or two.

Here is a reminder that although I am sometimes involved to some degree with the organization sometimes referred to as Nature-Loving Wonderland and at other times as Providence Maitreya or Maitreya Great Tao, of which you became a clergy member approximately in your early twenties, I am also involved with several other religious organizations and consider the competing guidelines, beliefs, and practices with a sense that the full reality may be beyond what any one of them can come anywhere close to fully expressing.

Happy Holidays! Season's Greetings!

Jim

------ Original Message ------
Received: Wed, 19 Sep 2012 10:44:33 AM CDT
From: "Maurice J. Blair" <██████████████>
To: Yin-Hsuan Chiu <██████████████>
Subject: Re: Universal Family Watch

Sherry,

That's great! I plan to buy the watch this Sunday, September 23rd, at the temple.

Sincerely,

Jim

------ Original Message ------
Received: Tue, 18 Sep 2012 08:56:35 PM CDT
From: Yin-Hsuan Chiu <█████████████>
To: █████████████
Subject: Re: Universal Family Watch

Hi Jim,

Oh please disregard my previous email. In fact, Tsai Fo Yuan just arrived to Liang Tyan Temple today and she brought back the style you ordered ($22.00USD). So your watch is at the temple now. Welcome to pick it up anytime! Hope to see you all soon!!

Sincerely,

Sherry

On Tue, Sep 18, 2012 at 6:34 PM, Yin-Hsuan Chiu <█████████████> wrote:

> Hi Jim,
>
> This is Sherry from Liang Tyan Temple. How do you do?
>
> I've come back from visiting Taiwan and I indeed had a great time over
> there with many friends and family members!
> I also remembered to order the universal family / fortunate watches for
> the people who made the order. Unfortunately, the style that you picked,
> which is $22.00 USD is currently out of stock. We did not have it this
> time. If you like to take the same one, we will have to wait until Taiwan
> restocks and ship it over here. In the meanwhile, I've also brought back
> another option that I showed you before, which is on the picture that I
> attached to this email. You're also welcome to come to the temple any time
> to take a look. It is more expensive but it is great quality. It costs
> $65.00 USD. If you like it and cannot complete the payment at one time, we
> can do maybe $20.00 per month for you. Let me know! May Maitreya Buddha and
> the everlasting happiness bless you and your family & friends!
>
> This upcoming Sunday is another class session. (9/23)
> The last Sunday of this month (9/30) is the Moon Festival day. Liang Tyan
> Temple welcomes everyone to join both events starting at 11:30 a.m..
>
> Kindest Regards,
>
> Sherry
>

[68]

Maurice Blair < ██████████████ >   Mon, Dec 23, 2024 at 6:15 AM
To: Yin-Hsuan Chiu < ████████████ .tw>
Cc: Liza Darnton < ██████████████ >, Alex Tse < ████████████ .au>, Ry Pickard < ██████████████ >, Tad
Schmaltz <tschmalt@umich.edu>, Dan Nolan < ████████████ >, Ming Blair < ████████████ >

Sherry,

Although, if you and my mother wind up with different versions of what you had said to her, if anything, in relationship with what she had characterized you as having said, I might not ever know for sure in this worldly life how much of the accuracy was with whom, whatever happens next should prove at least somewhat enlightening.

Please take a look at the portion of the forwarded email that has her advising me to conduct myself with filial piety taken to the extreme, alleging you to have corroborated with advocacy for that sort of thing for people in general and/or for it to specially apply to your case as of then. After taking a look at that, please see whether you deem it best to exercise your right to remain silent or to exercise your right to go ahead and write something to me--either as part of hitting "reply all," composing, and sending, or by another means of communication--about your memory and reactions regarding it.

By the way, and this goes not only to you but also to the six cc line people, for clarification, in the forwarded message my statement involving my cousin Alex became typed before I added my mother to the list of cc line recipients in that prior communique. I intended originally only two to go on that cc line, then I changed my mind and added a third person to that line. Subsequently, I did not find and edit the line to correct that detail.
  Making that line fully accurate in its context, here is one version of what it would have otherwise stated: "Although my cousin Alex (who is among the first two on the cc line of this message) may find it awkward for me to mention it here, this can be illustrated by part of what happened recently during an argument with my mother Ming regarding several things with life in general and differences of choices."

Although I recognize that you might be disappointed to find that Providence Maitreya Buddha Missionary Institute did not receive any reference in the forwarded draft of a last will and testament, the way that things have unfolded such that this present message is happening does involve acknowledgment of the Nature Loving Wonderland / Providence Maitreya religious organization having been one of the many religious organizations to have had a meaningful and helpful effect on my life, especially my ability to help other sentient beings.

Thanks for your role in proving helpful. I look forward to either your chiming in with a response or remaining silent. Either way, have a great day!

On another note, as your father Sam seemed perhaps on the verge of knocking on heaven's door when he and I last met approximately half a year ago, I shall mention wishing your family the best regarding his situation, whether he is still currently among those remaining in this worldly life or he is among the dearly departed. Also, best wishes to others in your family!

Again, Season's Greetings!
Jim

---------- Forwarded message ---------
From: **Maurice Blair** < ████████████ >
Date: Sun, Dec 22, 2024 at 8:17 PM
Subject: Fwd: A 28 AUG 2024 DRAFT LAST WILL & TESTAMENT, BEFORE ADJUSTMENTS
To: Liza Darnton < ████████████ >, Dan Nolan < ████████████ >, Ry Pickard < ████████████ >
Cc: Tad Schmaltz <tschmalt@umich.edu>, Alex Tse < ████████████ .au>, Ming Blair < ████████████ >

Liza, Dan, and Ry,

The aftermath of sending this message will possibly help with several determinations: 1) which services, if any, I might in the future hire Kirkus to do; 2) which services, if any, I might in the future hire other providers of review and/or editing services to do; 3) whether I someday return to the traditional model of creating manuscripts with which to send to agents in hopes of reaching mass market publication, rather than the straight-to-micropublishing method which I have done

[69]

prodigiously in the past 27 months; 4) whether any and/or all of you might choose to take tangible steps toward swaying what I might decide in terms of determinations 1, 2, and 3.

It is surprising how much difficulty some people have with understanding my family sometimes. Here is an attempt to clarify such as to foster the improvement of lives in general:

* * * * *

After getting partway into Fall Semester 1994, early during my freshman year at Duke, inspired in part by the {starring David Carradine (1936-2009) as the protagonist} *Kung Fu* and *Kung Fu: The Legend Continues* TV series, in part by other popular cultural items, and, in very large part by the sometimes-mind-boggling and often-intriguing readings from the "Introduction to Philosophy" class that Dr. Schmaltz (who is among the cc line recipients of this message), a huge shift happened.

Specifically, it was similar to how some scenes from *Black Widow* (2021) involved variations of how mammals can sometimes deactivate visceral, strong affection--either in general or in specific relation to someone or something--and it was similar to how many religious ascetics have done similar ways of controlling some ranges of activating, deactivating, and reactivating that.

I had reached a way of using the mind to deconstruct the patterns of normal reality such that I could almost any time at-will turn on, turn off, or turn to some intermediate level affection for nearly anyone. It was crude early on, it sometimes went away entirely, there were rollercoasters of changes, and, in the long run, that ability became consistently capable and much more advanced.

In contrast with that, a popular practice among humankind is for males to have consistent, strong, and at-times indiscriminate affection toward females of whatever range would automatically appeal to those males' fancy. I used to be much that way, and I can still be that way to a limited degree early in the interactions with some females upon first meeting. Also, in platonic interactions with males and females, there is often at least a little element of this happening with my psyche. HOWEVER, as interactions proceed, no matter what anyone does in interactions, whether of any gender, any other demographic, of any rank, of any past accomplishments, or whatever, the fact that at the core level I have the ability to perceive it my duty to REALITY to flip the switch when it becomes evident that I should flip the switch on that. Therefore, no matter how much any combination of beings or any individual might believe himself, herself, itself, or themselves to be entitled to being beyond reproach based on demographics, accomplishments, rank, context, or anything else, I look straight toward THE ABSOLUTE (to whatever degree that IT/HE/SHE/THEY might turn out to be of any given religion(s), any given science(s), and/or any other anything(s), whether best referenced as "G-d," "God," "The Totality of Reality," "The Ultimate Reality," "The Primordial Awakened Consciousness," &c.) such that if the most up-to-date entirety of interaction no longer makes it justified for me to care very thoroughly about the other, than, no matter who the other person is, even a former romantic partner, then I can simply shut down any amount of the affection as if a mechanical device, out of a sincere belief that this is the correct way to serve soteriology. Although some of the people such as a few family members, friends, and acquaintances have found it baffling and perplexing, your pattern has been able to earn a consistently high level with that. To put this another way, although you might perceive that you have done only a modest amount to help my life, I believe and to some degree know that your choices at several key junctures were extraordinarily perfect in terms of helping my life, especially with respect to overcoming obstacles in general, both for my health and for my ability to help other beings.

Although my cousin Alex (who is among the two on the cc line of this message) may find it awkward for me to mention it here, this can be illustrated by part of what happened recently during an argument with my mother Ming regarding several things with life in general and differences of choices. In that I said to Mother Ming, "Look, although you have done much to help my life, you have also done much to harm my life. It's not like with my father, who helped my life tremendously--not perfectly, but still tremendously--and who caused only small amounts of harm to my life. With you, in contrast, it's sort of like a company that's only worth $100,000 in balance because it has something like $13 trillion of assets and only $100,000 less than $13 trillion in liabilities." This can be a sample of how people can relate to part of how Stephen R. Covey (1932-2012) and others modeled emotional bank accounts. My late father Maurice A.T. Blair (1931-2015), of course, had what some would consider extreme warping from his combat experiences in Korea and Vietnam, plus the way that many civilians in America acted in portions of the late 1960s to mid-1970s.

* * * * *

That being said, here is something I have been holding back for years and years from disclosing to the one of you with the name Liza, and which the others of you probably had little or no knowledge regarding, presented as a direct message within this:

Liza, You probably noticed when about one-and-a-half decades ago I notified you by a direct one-to-one message on Facebook that my former upstairs neighbor, Barbara Hawkins (1945-2013), was at times showing signs of not feeling very great with life, given her divorce and other factors, and that she had told me that long ago she was the president of the Duke chapter of Alpha Phi (around the middle of the 1960s). Remembering that you mentioned that you joined Alpha Phi when you and I were discussing Psi Upsilon and other organizations and other stuff, I suggested that maybe you might arrange for a few Alpha Phi Sorority sisters to visit Barbara, perchance to comfort her and help her get better. Although you did not direct message me back about that idea, I have wondered many times in recent years about whether Barbara might have told you what my mother indicated that Barbara told her about the following: Barbara Hawkins perceived Maurice A.T. Blair as having stripped his wife Ming Blair of her femininity, according to accounts and descriptions that Ming Blair told me several times. I have known my mother and my father well enough to be able to tell that the truth is much more intricate than that crude oversimplification. Ming Blair was greatly affected by how her parents were closely involved with the Chinese side of World War II and the Capitalist side of the Chinese Civil War, then fled to Taiwan as part

[70]

of that Capitalist side. Also, she was affected by many other things besides my father's extremely militaristic influence. When mainstream culture presents things like a son or a daughter considering that descendant's mother as somehow "dearest" or "the primary early source of comfort and support" that is something that to which I can relate by attempting to put myself in their shoes, but it is not at all something that I have felt on any other than the rarest of occasions. Yes, my mother's aneurysm when I was about seven months old and its aftermath are part of why, my mother's growing up in a military family is part of why, my father's militarism was part of why, etc. She sometimes and to some degree cares for people in ways that exhibit significant degrees of femininity, but oftentimes people with sustained and repeated direct contact with her tend to find her to have those tendencies much more curbed than many females. Barbara's idea on this was somewhat overblown in some ways, besides being also a major oversimplification. As this e-mail is part of the sets of forerunners for if and when I might someday compose a full-length autobiography with which to send to literary agents (and perhaps to go unpublished in my lifetime or perhaps go published in my lifetime), here is something insightful that will also possibly disturbing: Ming has told me on multiple occasions, when trying to persuade me to choose to agree more with her on things that I would otherwise disagree, that she believes in an extreme ideal of how descendants would exhibit filial piety, whereas I believe filial piety should be in moderation and should look out for proper tradeoffs with all other types of piety. That is one of the main issues that makes the situation sometimes difficult, besides how she declines to run her online use of accounts, even her email account, shifting all of that responsibility to me since after my father passed on and became no longer available to run my mother's accounts for her, and besides how the nearest known relatives in contact are in California, Hong Kong, and Taiwan, too far away to pick up part of the burden of taking care of her. On another note, my October 1, 2022 e-mail message to you included typing from memory a statement that subtly and unintentionally misstated part of what Dale Carnegie (1888-1955) had stated *How to Win Friends and Influence People*. From memory, the description was that an editor had told Carnegie that he could tell right away from writings that some people were not going to be popular as writers because they lacked genuine interest in other people, whereas sometime circa mid-2023 I revisited part of that book and found that the actual statement was that an editor had told Carnegie that he could tell right away from writings that some people were not going to be popular as writers because they lacked sufficiently liking people. Something that correcting that characterization makes me think about is that an extraordinary number of times in my life many people have imposed very much on me to avoid liking very many people very much, based on the idea that it would be unethical, impractical, or, for whatever other reason(s), inappropriate. Some of that is readily apparent in much of my writing: over and over again dealing with strong impositions from others to curb or eliminate the liking people within many ranges.

* * * * *

Back to addressing all three of the to-line recipients.
    Part of the difficulty is exhibited by the following conversational sample, approximating a type of conversation that has happened multiple times. It involves reference to an Asian woman named Sherry, who graduated from college circa 2010, and her father Sam. Bear in mind that it is uncertain to me whether and to what degree my mother might have materially distorted at least one or two elements of something that Sherry had told her.

Ming: You know that Sherry told me that she is so loyal to her father that if he told her to commit suicide, then she would kill herself, no questions asked.

Jim: This is ridiculous! Blind obedience of that kind is way too much! I do not for sure whether suicide is ever ethical, and if it is, then it is probably only in very limited ranges.

Ming: That's the kind of loyalty that I had toward my parents. You should have that kind of loyalty to ancestors.

Jim: No! I disagree. If my father was still alive, I'm quite sure he would agree with me on this. Maybe the U2 pilot who got shot down in Russia might have better committed suicide as it was what the military guideline for him was in that case in the Cold War, but in the vast majority of cases it seems preposterous to impose on someone that the person go straight into blind obedience to commit suicide on command. This line of thinking is reminiscent of the 1962 version of *The Manchurian Candidate*, which my father and I watched in early 2000 or thereabouts.

* * * * *

As a last-minute adjustment I decided to add my mother's email address on the cc line. Although she arranges for me to run that account for her, I make sure to be responsible with informing her of any important messages received, and I make sure to only send messages from her account with her consent, knowledge, and direct involvement with the craftsmanship of the messages. It is extraordinarily rare for her to send messages to people, in large part because it takes two people for her to send such a message, with me performing all of her typing, since her arthritis and other factors she uses to be justification to usually completely avoid even touching computer keyboards and computer mice. In this case, I will plan to print out the message and hand her a copy, in order that she can study it at her own pace.

On another note, I have not completely finalized that last will and testament.

It is uncertain whether I might hire Bowker, Kirkus, Kevin Anderson & Associates, or another organization someday for professional editing service(s).

Whatever the case may be, stuff like this can be prime candidates for future nonfiction that I might place within manuscripts to send to agents, whether any of you particularly like it or not. Some parts of the Internet indicate that random people from the general public only get about one manuscript out of six thousand to achieve big-time, mainstream, large-scale publication with major publishers.

I choose to carry virtually no illusions about anyone or anything, because the toughness of life has led me to believe that I generally do not have the right to illusions, except for unintentional and/or inescapable ones, under penalty of nearly unlimited horror from the beyond.

By the way, in a separate communication, I clarified a few months ago to Steve Raynor (who evidently went by "S. T-Bone Raynor" when briefly running for political office in 2022) that instead of "Central Tibetan Authority" in the draft, it should have stated, "Central Tibetan Administration."

Kind Regards, Happy Holidays, and Season's Greetings!
Jim Blair

---------- Forwarded message ---------
From: **Maurice Blair** <███████████████>
Date: Sun, Dec 22, 2024 at 1:02 AM
Subject: Fwd: A 28 AUG 2024 DRAFT LAST WILL & TESTAMENT, BEFORE ADJUSTMENTS
To: Steve Raynor <████████████████████>, Dan Nolan <████@kirkus.com>, Ry Pickard
<████@kirkus.com>

---------- Forwarded message ---------
From: **Maurice Blair** <███████████████>
Date: Wed, Aug 28, 2024 at 3:46 PM
Subject: Re: A 28 AUG 2024 DRAFT LAST WILL & TESTAMENT, BEFORE ADJUSTMENTS
To: Stephen Raynor <██████████████████>

Stephen,

In accordance with your request, and providing more than the request for information relevant, here is an extended and edited version of the list in stipulation #11:

‾‾
a. 2% (i.e., one part out of fifty).
International Campaign for Tibet
1825 Jefferson Place NW
Washington, DC 20036
https://savetibet.org/

‾‾
b. 0.2% (i.e., one part out of five hundred).
Duke University Annual Fund
Box 90600
Durham, NC 27708
https://giving.duke.edu/annual-fund/about-the-duke-annual-fund/

‾‾
c. 0.1% (i.e., one part out of one thousand).
Baylor University
Waco, TX 76798
https://www.baylor.edu/

‾‾
d. 0.2% (i.e., one part out of five hundred).
McCombs School of Business
The University of Texas at Austin
2110 Speedway
Austin, TX 78712
https://www.mccombs.utexas.edu/

e. Liza Darnton: 1% (i.e., one part out of one hundred). (If she predeceases me, then her next of kin would substitute for her.)

X handle as of August 2024: @LizaDarnton.

If an executor has difficulty reaching her directly or her closest of next of kin directly, please bear in mind that her father and her brother-in-law were somewhat famous in some circles as of the 2020s, and, therefore, agents of some of her relatives might be helpful with that process.

f. The United States of America in such a way as to pay down the national debt and/or build toward a national surplus: 0.2% (i.e., one part out of five hundred). (separate from any tax obligations).

("Gifts to reduce the debt held by the public"). (Cf. https://www.treasurydirect.gov/government/public-debt-reports/gifts/.)

g. 0.1% (i.e., one part out of one thousand).
Rice University
6100 Main St.
Houston, TX 77005
rice.edu

h. 0.1 % (i.e., one part out of one thousand).
The University of Pennsylvania
Philadelphia, PA 19104
https://www.upenn.edu/

i. The Republican Party (of the United States of America): 1% (i.e., one part out of one hundred).
Republican National Committee
310 First Street SE
Washington D C 20003

j. The Libertarian Party (of the United States of America): 0.1% (i.e., one part out of one thousand).
Libertarian National Committee
1444 Duke St
Alexandria, VA 22314

k. The Democratic Party (of the United States of America): 0.2% (i.e., one part out of five hundred).
Democratic National Committee
430 South Capitol St SE #3
Washington, DC 20003

l. The Green Party (of the United States of America): 0.1% (i.e. one part out of one thousand).
The Green Part of the United States
PO Box 75075
Washington, DC 20013

m. 1% (i.e., one part out of one hundred).
True Buddha Foundation
17110 NE 40th CT, Redmond
WA 98052, USA.

(This portion should probably be delivered by check to it or by another careful method to make sure it is really to it and not an individual involving it, because one time in 2023 I did what I thought was a wire transfer to it - via an instruction on its web page to invite people to send money directly to an account for Lu Sheng-Yen (a.k.a. Grand Master Sheng-Yen Lu) - but it turned out that they counted it as a personal gift to Grand Master Sheng-Yen Lu himself, therefore telling me that the wire transfer would not count as a tax deductible donation.)

n. Whoever the Director of the Internal Revenue Service Is As of The Time of My Death: 0.01% (i.e., one part out of ten thousand). (Address to be determined).
related addresses as of August 28, 2024:

[73]

IRS:
irs.gov.
Department of the Treasury:
treasury.gov.

---

o. 0.1% (i.e., one part out of one thousand).
The Sheng-Yen Lu Foundation
17102 NE 40th Court Redmond, WA 98052 U.S.A.
https://sylfoundation.org/

---

p. Frank McDonald II (who was an elementary school classmate in portions of the 1980s in Ysletta Independent School District, and who later connected with me on some portions of online social media): 0.5% (i.e., one part out of two hundred). (If he predeceases me, then his next of kin would substitute for him.)
X handle as of August 2024: @FMcDonald_JDS. As of some portions of the 2020s he worked for Socorro Independent School District.

---

q. Whoever the Director of the FBI Is As of the Time of My Death: 0.04% (i.e., one part out of two thousand five hundred). (Address to be determined).
related address as of August 28, 2024:
Federal Bureau of Investigation
fbi.gov.

---

r. 0.1% (i.e., one part out of one thousand).
KTLA-TV
5800 Sunset Blvd.
Los Angeles, CA 90028
https://ktla.com/

---

s. 0.1% (i.e., one part out of one thousand).
News Radio KTRH
1233 West Loop South
Suite 725
Houston, TX 77027
https://ktrh.iheart.com/

---

t. 0.2% (i.e., one part out of five hundred).
International Association of Scientologists
4751 Fountain Ave.
Los Angeles, CA 90029, USA
https://iasmembership.org/

---

u. 0.1% (i.e., one part out of one thousand).
Citizens Commission on Human Rights
6616 Sunset Blvd
Los Angeles, California 90028
https://www.cchr.org/

Regards,
Maurice James Blair

On Wed, Aug 28, 2024 at 12:21 PM Stephen Raynor < ███████████████████ > wrote:
Excellent.

On Wed, Aug 28, 2024 at 12:10 PM Maurice Blair < ██████████████ > wrote:

[74]

Steve,

Please consider this draft and what some of the proper adjustments might be. BTW, I would like to see if we might be able to find a way to legally make the adjusted version binding without adding any more names to it than what it shows. That includes how it painstakingly uses categories in some cases to sidestep what might otherwise have been the outright spelling out of additional names.

A 28th Day of August 2024 Draft of What Maurice James Blair (as born an American Citizen by blood in Taiwan on June 14, 1976) Intends for His Last Will and Testament, to be adjusted into Legaleze within a Moderate Amount of Changing After Its Composition

1. All financial accounts that have valid reference to beneficiaries (whether Payable On Death, Transferable On Death, etc.), if any, who are still alive after I die shall go to those beneficiaries in accordance with their registrations, without anyone being able to legally contest otherwise.

2. Any real estate, if any, involved with joint ownership with another person should have my portion become inherited by the surviving person(s), if any, of the joint ownership. In the absence of such joint ownership with any surviving person as of the time of death, such real estate is to go to my closest surviving next of kin. If there is a tie for whom the claim to "closest surviving next of kin" would be, then it should go pro rata on an equal basis to each tying claimant. (Any subsequent descriptions in this document to "closest surviving next of kin" are also subject to this provision.) (For certain contingencies of disputes, please refer to stipulation #9.)

3. Any automobile, if any, of my sole ownership should go to the closest surviving next of kin.

4. Real estate, if any, of my sole ownership should go to the closest surviving next of kin.

5. Automobile(s), if any, of joint ownership should have my portion go to the surviving person(s), if any, of the joint ownership.

6. If I own shares of Synapsid Revelations Press Corporation at the time of my death, then those shares should go to Liza Darnton (who attended a philosophy class as one of my classmates in the Spring Semester of 1995, and who later became part of my LinkedIn network concomitant with my later becoming part of her LinkedIn network). With those shares, of course, go the royalties on any books registered for that corporation to receive royalties. (Of course, with this goes access to the safe deposit box(es), if any, registered for that corporation. However, such deposit box(es) should already have in them notes making clear which items within them are property of Synapsid Revelations Press Corporation and which items within them are my property. Therefore, there should be care to make sure that the appropriate items within those boxes go to the proper recipients; see stipulation #10 of this list.) If Liza Darnton predeceases me, then her next of kin are to receive those shares in her place.

7. Liza Darnton is also to receive the copyrights to the books published by Synapsid Revelations Press Corporation with myself as the author. If she predeceases me, then her next of kin are to receive those copyrights in my place.

8. If I have more than one residence at which I keep my nonautomobile personal property, then the executors should discuss with appropriate persons which of such property was solely possessed by me, which such property was jointly owned with others, etc. Any solely-owned property of that type should go to whomever else, if anyone, was a resident primarily of the place where it was at the time of my death. In the absence of anyone having primarily resided at such a place, my next of kin should negotiate among themselves who should inherit what among those items. If such next of kin should enter a dispute about who should inherit what with that, then they should face off in a nonphysically-threatening duel contest in their determination of at least one competition among 1) tennis (via a three-set match), 2) table tennis (via an old-school first to reach twenty-one points contest), 3) chess (via a match consisting of at least four games), 4) poker (by five card draw with a traditional 52-card modern deck, with officials carefully preventing anything other than a fair competition of it), 5) flipping a coin (of exactly or almost exactly 50%-50% chances for heads and tails), observed officially and adjudicated by the executor of the will if the executor is not among the disputants. If the executor of the will is among the disputants, then the next of kin of Frank McDonald II should serve as the official observer and judge. If Frank McDonald II is still alive as of that time, then he should determine which of his next of kin would serve in that capacity. If the determined person does not feel qualified to be such an observer and judge, then that person shall be assigned to designate anyone appropriate of that person's choice to be the objective third party to serve in that role. If the next person up does not feel qualified, then that person is to designate another person. This process can proceed through whatever number of people would be needed to arrive at a resolution. If the executor of the estate determines there to have occurred too many rounds of designated people sidestepping considering themselves qualified, then the executor could call off that process, replacing it with a simple resolution in which any basically competent and objective adult can observe a simple drawing of a single Tarot card by each dueling person from a randomly shuffled Oswald Wirth Tarot Deck, with high

card winning, in accordance with the following basis in this case: 1) Each Major Arcana card outranks any of the Minor Arcana cards. 2) Card XXI of the Major Arcana ranks highest, and the other 77 cards proceed in rank in descending order, with Card XX ranking second, with Card I as the penultimate in the order (i.,e., second to last / second to lowest in rank among those) and Card 0 as the lowest in that arcana. 3) Of the Minor Arcana the Aces rank highest, Kings second highest, Queens third, Knights fourth, and Pages fifth, Ten ranking sixth, and the remainder proceeding in descending order, with the Deuces last / lowest ranking. 4) In this case the four suits shall be given a ranking (in case of what would otherwise be an Ace-vs.-Ace tie, a 10-vs.-10 tie, etc.) of Swords highest ranked, Cups second ranked, Wands third ranked, and Coins fourth ranked. Therefore, the Two (i.e., Deuce) of Coins would be the lowest ranking card in that setup, whereas XXI. The World would be the highest ranking card in that setup.

9. If any disputes among heirs and/or attempted heirs occur and appear to otherwise be headed for costly legal disputes in a court of law or multiple courts of law regarding the carrying out of any potential disputes other than those described for resolution in stipulation #8, then, rather than fully utilizing such courts, the dispute resolution technique outlined in stipulation #8 should be utilized for them.

10. As part of facilitating stipulation #6, prior to separating which property within Synapsid Revelations Press Corporation's safe deposit box(es), if any, should go to whom, any person opening the box(es) should utilize sufficient videorecording and/or presence of witnesses to facilitate reasonable confidence among affected parties that the proceedings are happening properly. This might require extra care in negotiating with the bank(s) and/or others exactly how the proceedings can happen.

11. If as of the time of my death I have any nonretirement (i.e., bank accounts, brokerage accounts, etc. other than IRAs, etc.) financial accounts that lack any designated beneficiary, such that the financial institutions have no clear guidance on distribution/transfer upon my death, and/or if there are any nonretirement financial accounts for which any and all designated beneficiary/beneficiaries is/are already deceased prior to my death, then the distribution of those fund should be in accordance with the percentages detailed as follows:
a. International Campaign for Tibet: 2% (i.e., one part out of fifty).
b. Duke University: 0.2% (i.e., one part out of five hundred).
c. Baylor University: 0.1% (i.e., one part out of one thousand).
d. The University of Texas at Austin: 0.2% (i.e., one part out of five hundred).
e. Liza Darnton: 1% (i.e., one part out of one hundred). (If she predeceases me, then her next of kin would substitute for her.)
f. The United States of America in such a way as to pay down the national debt and/or build toward a national surplus: 0.2% (i.e., one part out of five hundred). (separate from any tax obligations).
g. Rice University: 0.1% (i.e., one part out of one thousand).
h. The University of Pennsylvania (at Philadelphia): 0.1 % (i.e., one part out of one thousand).
i. The Republican Party (of the United States of America): 1% (i.e., one part out of one hundred).
j. The Libertarian Party (of the United States of America): 0.1% (i.e., one part out of one thousand).
k. The Democratic Party (of the United States of America): 0.2% (i.e., one part out of five hundred).
l. The Green Party (of the United States of America): 0.1% (i.e. one part out of one thousand).
m. True Buddha School Foundation: 1% (i.e., one part out of one hundred). (This portion should probably be delivered by check to it, because one time in 2023 I did what I thought was a wire transfer to it, but it turned out that they counted it as a personal gift to Grand Master Sheng-Yen Lu himself, therefore telling me that the wire transfer would not count as a tax deductible donation.)
n. Whoever the Director of the Internal Revenue Service Is As of The Time of My Death: 0.01% (i.e., one part out of ten thousand).
o. The Sheng-Yen Lu Foundation: 0.1% (i.e., one part out of one thousand).
p. Frank McDonald II (who was an elementary school classmate in portions of the 1980s, and who later connected with me on some portions of online social media): 0.5% (i.e., one part out of two hundred).
q. Whoever the Director of the FBI Is As of the Time of My Death: 0.04% (i.e., one part out of two thousand five hundred).
r. The television station KTLA: 0.1% (i.e., one part out of one thousand).
s. The radio station KTRH: 0.1% (i.e., one part out of one thousand).
t. International Association of Scientologists: 0.2% (i.e., one part out of five hundred).
u. Citizens Commison on Human Rights: 0.1% (i.e., one part out of one thousand).
v. My Next of Kin: The remaining residual (i.e., 93%, in other words, ninety-three parts out of one hundred). (However, portions of that may need to go toward paying taxes.)

12. The United States Federal Bureau of Investigation (hereafter referred to as "the FBI") is to be granted by my cellphone and email account providers (if any) full access to my cellphone and email records. The FBI is to also determine which portion(s) if any of that information would be appropriate to disclose to my next of kin and/or other persons. If the FBI no longer exists at the time of my death, then the United States Central Intelligence Agency (hereafter referred to as "the CIA") is to receive such access in its place. If neither the FBI nor the CIA exist as of the time of my death, then the executor of the estate is to decide to whom access to those records should be granted.

13. The Central Tibetan Authority (hereafter referred to as "the CTA") is to be granted by my social media providers full access to my social media accounts. The CTA is also to determine which portion(s) if any of that information would be appropriate to disclose to my next of kin and/or other persons. If the CTA no longer exists as of that time or declines to obtain such access, then such access is to be granted to Duke University. If Duke University no longer exists as of that time or declines to obtain such access, then such access is to be granted to The University of Texas at Austin. If The University of Texas at Austin no longer exists as of that time or declines to obtain such access, then the executor of the estate is to decide to whom access to those records should be granted.

14. If any retirement accounts lack designated beneficiaries, then 2% of them are to go to International Campaign for Tibet, 3% of them are to go to Liza Darnton (or, if she predeceases me, then her next of kin), 1% to Frank McDonald II (or, if he predeceases me, then his next of kin), and 94% of them are to go to my next of kin.

15. My next of kin and whichever organizations might obtain access to informative accounts via stipulation #12 and/or stipulation #13 are to be reasonably cooperative with Liza Darnton (or her next of kin if she predeceases me) and my next of kin, in order to facilitate interactions helpful toward the future of sentient beings. If they decide to decline to cooperate at all, then the beings with whom they decline to cooperate are to use any and all means they deem appropriate to convert that lack of cooperation into usefully becoming part of facilitating interactions helpful toward the future of sentient beings.

16. If the telephone provider(s), email providers, and social media providers wind up obstructing the fulfilment of stipulation #12 and/or stipulation #13 and/or stipulation #15, then anyone named and/or otherwise identified by this will shall hereby be encouraged to use any and all means deemed appropriate to help foster the future of the enlightenment of sentient beings.

17. My next of kin are to inherit any copyrights to which I am both the copyright office claimant and the publisher (in contrast with the items described by stipulation #7). They are also to inherit any royalties from those works.

18. The executor is to make sure to facilitate for the fulfilment of stipulations #6, #7, and #17 to include proper dissemination of computer files supportive of the future processes, if any, involved with the related publishing activities.

19. If the heirs who receive in accordance with stipulations #6, #7, and #17 sell rights to any stories to be converted into movies, then they are hereby encouraged, though not required, to arrange that some consultation with at least five persons in total and/or at least two organizations in total from the list consisting of the following would be involved with that process: The list from stipulation #11 plus The Church of Jesus Christ, Scientist (also referred to as the main Christian Science organization), The Methodist Church, The Drukpa Church of Nepal, The Philadelphia Seminar on Christian Origins, Houston Zen Center, Holocaust Museum Houston, The Smithsonian Institution (as was located in the District of Columbia as of 2024), and, last but not least, the Tibetan Buddhist Rimé Institute (as was located in Australia as of 2024).

20. Anyone who might ever encounter this will and/or its draft hereby receives a proclamation of encouragement to do whatever such persons and organizations might be able to do to help with the soteriology with which to transform a given reality into a better reality.

Regards,

Maurice James Blair

P.S. Please keep in some version of the extra verbiage in 11(m), because it opens the door to the possibility that, even though I choose much loyalty to TBS, if the IRS deems it appropriate to audit and argue with TBS about the procedure by which TBS managed the record keeping aftermath of that wire transfer (and how it presumably has in recent years managed the record keeping of similar such wire transfers), then I can fulfill my duty to REALITY to alert the IRS about that situation. That is also part of why I insist on 11(n) being adjacent to 11(m), to make extra sure that this opens the door to any relevant, appropriate, extra consideration of options by any affected organizations. Also, I reserve the right to accelerate the alerting of people and organizations about this or whatever else, by if I, for example, copy this message to becoming part of some yet-to-be-determined future publication, devoid of identifying which attorney and law office to whom I am sending it (for your privacy). Alternatively, with a similar m.o., I might copy some excerpts of it to some yet-to-be-determined future publication(s). I trust how TBS personnel responded to me about that situation, yet I remembered that a tax CPE course years ago indicated some preacher attempted an in-person method similar to that online procedure, and a tax court later ruled him to have received those payments not as tax-free gifts from the congregation, but as taxable income to himself.

STEPHEN JAMES RAYNOR
Attorney and Counselor at Law
6440 North Central Expressway
Suite 510
Dallas, TX 75206
(214) 821-1641

A 7-8 JANUARY 2025 Note Regarding the law firm notice: Since I was the client for that, I had the right and have the right, within a reasonable range, to forward that otherwise-confidential information to others, such as you, at my discretion. – Maurice J. Blair

Now, for something different, on the remainder of this page is a set of patterns:

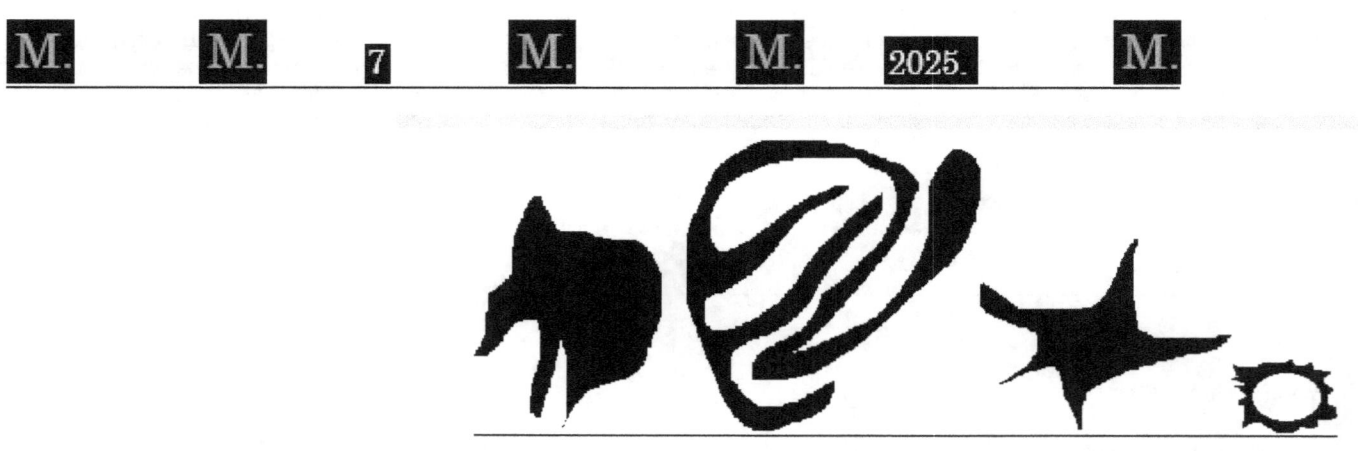

- Thursday, January 2, 2025 C.E.
- Saturday, January 4, 2025 C.E.
- Monday, January 6, 2025 C.E.
- Tuesday, January 7, 2025 C.E.
- Wednesday, January 8, 2025 C.E.

[78]

Some people talk about how the designers of Persian rugs would typically act out a tradition of intentionally placing a few "imperfections" into their construction, based on how this could relate to the mysteries of divinity such as to in some ways achieve a "more holistic perfection" by that intent than they would by attempting to achieve some variation of technically, most- perfectly pleasing those who would prefer absolutely-pedantic, completely-standards-based perfection. Yes, some manufacturers have considered "some possible technical imperfections" to be "among a form of higher-order super-perfections," at least to a modest degree within some contexts.

Whichever "technical imperfections" may have ever involved any amounts of unconsciousness, semiconsciousness, consciousness, or whatever else, we may often never know for sure when we read the literary works of others. In some cases, a publisher may even choose upon studying a proof to convert what had been an unconscious and unintentional anomaly during a late stage into becoming a conscious and intentional anomaly at the final stage in order to facilitate superior efficiency and provision of the presence of anomalies; this is in a similar vein to what some rugmaking traditions sometimes utilize.

Consider this: A transfiguration to *The Dimetrodons, the Dorians, and the Modern World, Synapsid Critical Edition* (2024) performed mentally such as to standardize several portions (beyond overtly shown text) would be to:

1) Take the "n" in "An Tale" on p. vii and teleport it to the "winnig" on p. 54, to show "A Tale" on p. vii and "winning" on p. 54.

2) Removing the "t" from "headintg" on p. 59, letting "heading" remain there, changing it to an "r," and teleporting it to the front of "esembling" on p. 74 to make that become "resembling."

3) Replacing the 5.5 and the 8.5 on p. 115 with 6 and 9 (i.e., trading away that digest-size reference to replace it with a trade-size reference regarding the pages size setting of *The Dimetrodons, the Dorians, and the Modern World: Revised Edition* (2022)).

Also, consider this: According to Internet records accessed in 2024, the 2001 C.E./A.D. reference about halfway down p. 113 of *The Dimetrodons, the Dorians, and the Modern World: Revised Edition* was an attempt to refer to 2002 C.E./A.D.

The preceding discussion serves, among other things, as a way of to some degree honoring portions of esoteric thoughts over the extreme persnickety hostility some literati may harbor against anything other than clean copy or almost clean copy. Indian, Mesopotamian, Persian, Greek, Sri Lankan, Chinese, Tibetan, and American esoteric thoughts may sometimes go into that issue of various oriental rugs, occidental rugs, northern rugs, southern rugs, central rugs, jugs, mugs, thugs, bugs, plugs, drugs, hugs, travel logs, and freedom from drugs. For example, contrast portions of *The Larger Prajnaparamita-Hridaya Sutra* (also known as "The Long Version" of *The Heart Sutra*) with instances of routine western civilization pedantic, picky, snap-judgment condemnation that can at times lead people to wrong conclusions, such as if and when people go overboard with the idea structures on the strict Walker side of guidance mentioned on p. 54 of this *Shape Up or Ship Out* nonfiction book. A middle way between the aforementioned strict Walker side of guidance and the lax Schlesinger side of guidance mentioned on p. 55 is often warranted. A related discussion occurs on pp. 134-135 of *Alternative Beginnings and Endings of All Things: Science, Religion, Politics, and Cards, Hypervolume II* (2024).

From: Maurice Blair < >

Sent: Monday, December 23, 2024 12:01 PM

To: ███████ @fbi.gov>

Cc: Dan Nolan <███████@Kirkus.com>; Ry Pickard <███████@Kirkus.com>

Subject: Fwd: various

————— Forwarded message —————

From: Maurice Blair < >

Date: Sat, Dec 21, 2024 at 11:08 PM

Subject: Fwd: various

To: Dan Nolan <███████@kirkus.com>, Ry Pickard <███████@kirkus.com>, Steve Raynor < █████████████████████ >

Dan, Ry, and Steve,

In accordance with the best of ability to tell the totality of reality, I have decided to send you this message no matter what the unknown might be relative to the horizon of my knowledge. In other words, there is no reaction that you could make to this that would be compatible with my deciding to apologize to any of you for sending it.

Now, I shall address you with a degree of individuation. Each portion of that will be de facto a situation of having whoever is not directly addressed being as if on a cc line.

***

Steve,

The fact that you have gone silent for a very long time, since you found out that Justin Haynes had somewhat flipped out and that I had him dead cold with him on the wrong side of facts and me on the right side of facts, etc., is a factor.

Had you sent follow-up responses, then you might have had some type of bearing on influencing me in the direction of not including you in the set of communications of which this forwarding is the initial step. I still respect you to a degree, yet, as one of your clients--or past clients, still invited theoretically to hire you again--I have the right to publicly or semi-publicly identify you nearly at will.

Recently, although a review from Kirkus Reviews fit the range of merchantability as deemed by me, one of their indie clients, it opened up a door into multitudes of questions in mind about what was under the surface. Basically, the review was tantamount to fighting words. It is not my place as per their contract to make any very direct inquiry with them about whatever was happening behind closed doors or whatever with what led to the review. However, the review was exceedingly surprising to me, and it has already proven very useful due to factors that might become readily apparent to them as time goes by.

You might ask why I chose to have it published. For me there is no actual middle ground on this of an area where a merchantable review as deemed by me would be buried outside of being published. As expressed in various ways, I am a true believer that the sort of thing in *Ecclesiastes* 12, some versions of Abrahamic Religion(s) in general, and some versions of Dharmic Religion(s), including many expressions of Mahayana Buddhism, that in the long run there is nowhere to hide with respect to anything that any of us as sentient beings ever thinks, feels, speaks, writes, or acts. Therefore, for me to not select a review for publication, it would have to be so bad that I would go to some form of legal war against the reviewing entity and thereby wind up revealing it to others without the reviewing organization's consent anyway. and, although I found the recent review in some ways profoundly objectionable, I deemed it still well within the range of merchantability; and, in fact, humorous in several ways, a sort of unintentional comdedy.

It appears to me that you are not planning to bill me for anything beyond the initial $750 that I paid you by check when meeting you in Waco. That being said, part of what has occurred is that it appears very clear to me that whatever has been happening beyond the horizon of my knowledge at Kirkus Reviews has involved some degree of failure to sense the reality of much of what I have put into the nonfiction. Let there be no doubt about it, as referenced in other sets of words in *Alternative Beginnings and Endings of All Things*, I have for many years crafted each choice such that, to the best of my ability to discern, I am doing my utmost to keep things in ranges that I could thoroughly explain and defend in the eventuality of some future JUDGMENT DAY in any religion(s) and/or science fiction(s) that might turn out to later be actual, factual reality. Therefore, although they did not ask me to provide specific evidence of what was beyond the surface of *The Science, Religion, Politics, and Cards Trilogy*, I am bringing them into experiencing several portions of it, whether or not it winds up mending fences with them, or whatever else.

One of the things mentioned in both *Science, Religion, Politics, and Cards* and *Alternative Beginnings and Endings of All Things* was commitment to the bearing of true witness, as you are almost undoubtedly well aware by now. Also, I reported many cases of making examples out of people and organizations, both in some of my nonfiction literature and elsewhere. The way that I went through years of struggle as a patient of the psychiatric industry and later paid enough dues with REALITY to overcome challenges such as to extract myself completely from being a patient of that industry, thereby becoming a former patient of the psychiatric industry, was in many respects a baptism by blood, a baptism by apocalyptic experiences, and more. As long as it involves an honorable death, the issue of life-and-death that terrifies many people to the core is simply immaterial to me, as I have informed you multiple times and in multiple ways. I will probably omit you from some of the messages that ensue with the set of which this is the first, as you are not primarily involved with the issues, though your presence in some of the communications is helpful. Meanwhile, Kirkus Reviews is directly involved with the main issues, although that organization might prove to be less central to the issue than several other organizations, not the least of which may turn out to be Gray Reed & McGraw and The Wealth Enhancement Group. Yes, The Wealth Enhancement Group (as was located in Houston, TX, and ceased to exist in some respects with becoming acquired by The Wealth Enhancement Group) happening, yet the way the recent review took shape indicates that the acquiring firm might have inherited more than that for which it had bargained. Time will probably tell.

Regards, M.J.B.

***

Dan and Ry,

To be clear, I agree with how the recently-published review should stay as-is on account not only to accord with our contractual arrangement but also as a cultural artifact that people can analyze. Online reviews, whether by professionals or amateurs can easily be considered way off base by various authors, publishers, readers, and others, and I actually find your organization's review of *Alternative Beginnings and Endings of All Things*, as off-base as I believe it to be, not as far off-base as I consider your organization's reviews of Clarke & Baxter's *Sunstorm* (2005) and Clarke & Baxter's *Firstborn* (2008). That being said, that recent review has eventually led to my reaching a combined solution to do with this set of messages what I am doing, even if you go hardline against me the way that Emily Bull went against me in April 2023 before partially reconciling with me on February 22, 2024 (and as partially broadcast on March 15, 2024 and July 5, 2024 on *The Michael Berry Show*).

Although I do not know what in the world happened with your review process for the recently-published review of *Alternative Beginnings and Endings of All Things*, Ockham's Razor and other methods have led to my modeling near certainly that something went amiss behind my back with a fact-check process or something similar. Perhaps someone outside your organization and those whom you contract was the primary source of why things have led to where they are. About the only way that something amiss along those lines did not happen would be if this is a close parallel to the Tycho Magnetic Anomaly Moonbase dynamic in *2001: A Space Odyssey*, in which a degree of playful misdirection to the general public can help to shield the general public from how they might not be able to handle the truth in some cases. However, I have decided to send you this communication in a manner compatible with any and all of the possibilities unknown to me. (Cf. *Alternative Beginnings and Endings of All Things: Science, Religion, Politics, and Cards, Hypervolume II* (2024), pp. 96, 104, 448, 476, regarding when a "combined solution" arrives). Also, whether or not you are at or near the edge of a cliff, metaphorically speaking, relative to the entirety of reality itself, your organization is in at least a few ways near the edge of at least one cliff, so to speak.

Therefore, in the interests of steering you away from multiple cliffs and steering much of the rest of anyone impacted away from various cliffs, whether or not there turns out to be any future business relationship between you and me, I am conducting the set of forwardings of which this is the first.

If you choose to ban me from doing business with you in the future as a reaction to how I am performing these messages, then I expect to have no regret about it. If you choose to continue to consider me eligible to do business with you in the future, then I expect to have no regret about it.

To be clear, if you were to ban me in a reasonably tasteful and respectful manner, then I will probably simply walk away into the sunset relative to you. That being said, I hope you will tune into the better angels of your nature and wind up proceeding forward in a reasonably benevolent path, because, although I am ready for the full range

On Mon, Dec 23, 2024 at 11:15 AM Dan Nolan <█████@kirkus.com> wrote:

Hi there,

Thank you for reaching out! Since the review is completed, we're unable to make any changes to it. We consider all matters closed once the review is completed. Please let me know if you have any further questions for me!

Best,
Dan

From: Maurice Blair <mjblair2956@gmail.com>
Sent: Monday, December 23, 2024 12:01 PM
To: █████@fbi.gov>
Cc: Dan Nolan <█████@Kirkus.com>; Ry Pickard <█████@Kirkus.com>
Subject: Fwd: various

---------- Forwarded message ----------
From: Maurice Blair <█████████>
Date: Sat, Dec 21, 2024 at 11:08 PM
Subject: Fwd: various
To: Dan Nolan <█████@kirkus.com>, Ry Pickard <█████@kirkus.com>, Steve Raynor <stephenjamesraynorlaw@gmail.com>

Dan, Ry, and Steve,

In accordance with the best of ability to tell the totality of reality, I have decided to send you this message no matter what the unknown might be relative to the horizon of my knowledge. In other words, there is no reaction that you could make to this that would be compatible with my deciding to apologize to any of you for sending it.

to Ry, Liza, Marcus, David, Steve, info, Michael, dkroll, jreed, Rose, Johnny, Ming, Alex, Jennifer, info, hpd.communityaffairs, Jason, Dan ▾

Dan,

Did you bother to read through my correspondence? If you did, then you either forgot that I stated point blank that I am NOT REQUESTING any change to it or you failed to take me at my word!!!

If you had responded by stating something like, "We are apprised of the situation. Cheers!" then I would not be hostile. However, your message reflected one of several possibilities: 1) a failure to read through the correspondence, 2) a forgetting a key point of what I stated, or 3) a failure to take me at my word.

To any who encounter this and feel immediate animosity toward me for sending it, bear in mind the message expressed in the last three paragraphs.

Here is a refresher:

"To be clear, I agree with how the recently-published review should stay as-is on account not only to accord with our contractual arrangement but also as a cultural artifact that people can analyze. Online reviews, whether by professionals or amateurs can easily be considered way off base by various authors, publishers, readers, and others, and I actually find your organization's review of *Alternative Beginnings and Endings of All Things*, as off-base as I believe it to be, not as far off-base as I consider your organization's reviews of Clarke & Baxter's *Sunstorm* (2005) and Clarke & Baxter's *Firstborn* (2008)." - M.J.B., December 21, 2024, to Dan Nolan, Ry Pickard, and Stephen Raynor

Had you stated, "We are apprised of the situation. Cheers!" then I would have considered that respectful. I would have almost definitely not even bothered to send any direct response to it.

However, you wrote to me as if presuming disingenuousness, evidently stemming from one of the three possibilities mentioned earlier.

* * *

At this stage I no longer give a damn about if the Democratic Party goes extinct to be replaced by a suitable replacement liberal party much the way that the Republican Party replaced the Whig Party!!

If I count up all the disrespect toward the bearing of true witness and all the disrespect by the method of the bearing of false witness, even though the Republican Party has not been all that great, the total vitriol either directly or indirectly aimed at me, my family, my religious affiliations, those outside my affiliations yet clearly railroaded, etc., as indicated by personal experience, news, TV, radio, the Internet, etc., has the full energy associated with the Democratic Party serving as an affront at several times as much as the Republican Party!!

Although I cheered for the best in a spirit of agnosticism--whether a Democratic victory in the 2024 general election or a Republican victory in the 2024 general election--recently, in accordance with the plan mentioned in *Alternative Beginnings and Endings of All Things*, and although I recognize *both the Democratic Party and the Republican Party to be dangerous in their own ways*, also as per what I stated in that book, I decided that the best I could tell from all available information, a Republican victory in that would probably be best. I voted that way, it turned out that way, and I have no regret about it.

   To help anyone seeing this understand, here is a simple analogy: You are on a team that has to make one move per round, and you get to vote for what move your team will make. The team could be analogous to the human race, America, all sentient beings, etc. Therefore, you vote for what you perceive to be best, yet not every single time you vote do you feel anywhere near entirely sure. If you feel uncertain, then you could cheer for the best choice while logically agnostic toward whether your specific vote is on the best side. When I voted I felt quite unsure. Now, the uncertainty is much smaller. I still have a trace of agnosticism toward this, but just in the past few days I have moved very much toward the right, and your choice to write to me in the manner in which you did is the straw that broke the camel-that-held-the-levee-together's back. The levee has broken.

Now, it is also possible that it might be best for *both the Republican Party and the Democratic Party to go away and get replaced by a new pair of parties*. I do not rule that out in the long run.

I care about soteriology, which I believe a properly functioning First Amendment and a reasonably-liberty-filled U.S. can help very much, yet there are reasons for a degree of skepticism toward both major political parties. That being said, the Republican Party has given my family personally much more reason for confidence than has the Democratic Party. I respect that someone with a very different set of life experiences could think and feel exactly the opposite way. I also covered this in *Alternative Beginnings and Endings of All Things*.

Some, including Marcus Padow, whom I have included with this message may perhaps question and/or condemn that I am revealing one of his FBI email addresses to a bunch of people via this message. However, the patterns of extreme, repeated disrespect from many people and organizations ever since the instant that Steve Estrin threatened that if I were to ever defeat a FinGroup client in serious chess that I would be fired, the patterns of extreme disrespect starting with that very instant have been terrible.

However, the patterns, as viewed holistically, have helped serve enlightenment well, as I have fought back time and time again. Several times I thought, *No need to complain any more about Steve Estrin, Natasha McDaniel, Juan Martinez, Michael Kelsheimer, and all that pattern from before; I've defeated that pattern well enough, and, as the old saying goes, There's no need to beat a dead horse*. However, clearly much of that problem or what emanates from adjacent to that problem persists.

This shall probably be clearer to at least a few of those on this list as there are more forwardings to come.

If Marcus were to attack me for daring to do this, then in the absence of my expressing the following, he might go down the same path he did on a wintry day in the Raleigh-Durham area in the mid-1990s; however, I shall point out differences.

A social member of Psi Upsilon, a woman named Laura Fitzpatrick, was driving a vehicle in which both Marcus and I were passengers. The road was slick due to ice. A wreck ensued. When the police arrived, I briefly cracked a wisecrack joke, thinking it would be funny in the situation. Marcus immediately scolded me, as it was not the correct time for humor. I took that to heart, though I have frequently, nevertheless, been far from perfect since then.

Here is the contrast:

In this case, I am deadly serious. Since I have not encountered any indication from Marcus that I should do anything other than use my own critical thinking, intuition, and such to decide to whom to reveal at least one of his email addresses, and due to the outrageous degree of disrespect that a few segments of American conservatism and many segments of American liberalism have done to me and my family in recent years, I have decided, based on all available factors, that it is best to compose this message exactly as I am composing it and to send it exactly as I am sending it.

When I composed *Of Dorians, Romans, Hebrews, Whigs, Democrats, Republicans, Indians, and Beyond* (2022, nonprofit/educational booklet, extremely limited distribution; unknown whether any unauthorized modified copies are in circulation besides the authorized unmodified copies; reprinted in 2023 with de minimis authorized modifications), I stopped short of outright stating my thought that it could very well be best for the Democratic Party to go extinct the way the Whig Party did, to be replaced by a better liberal party. However, things changed such that I have now stopped suppressing myself from putting that into writing. That having been stated, I spoke the idea out loud on rare occasions with a few people here and there in portions of late 2021, early 2022, and a few other times, most often by way of saying that it is what Mark R. Levin seems to think best, but that I am not entirely sold on it. However, things have changed. It appears to me at least a 20%-50% probability now.

On the other hand, maybe there are paths forward for the Democratic Party to shape up rather than ship out.

Whatever the case may be, whomever might study the additional forwardings will probably have a better idea. Any of you, even the two on the set of the "to" line and the "cc" line whom I respect the most, viz. Liza Darnton and Marcus Padow, choose to complain to me about how I am conducting this communication, I expect to have no regret about any of it, because the level of insult from various people is such that I am prepared to not even regret this if it were to cause human extinction to happen within 35 seconds after sending it. Actually, let's change that: within one second afterward. See, if anyone with the normal range of capabilities goes toward complaining, compare your plan of complaint or your actual complaint with human extinction within one second after it. When I expressed in many places about "Death before dishonor," I have meant it all the way to every possible instant human extinction. "Life together with honor," that is priceless, but sometimes if one has to go, and a person decides on something being a hill worth dying on, then life can wind up being much more sacrificeable.

Even if you are smug about the idea that it would be impossible, I advise you to let go of your smugness on that and try to understand what I am stating. I genuinely believe in a variety of religious aspects and/or mysterious advanced technological aspects of reality, in large part from utterly surreal experiences, and I am confident that it is very probable that every person will have to in the long run face a situation of nowhere to hide with respect to the totality of their lives relative to whatever the higher power(s) might turn out to be.

When I mentioned repeatedly in *The Science, Religion, Politics, and Cards Trilogy* an absolute commitment to a duty to reality, I meant every word of that.

Regards,
Maurice James Blair

...

<u>A January 9, 2025 Note About that December 23, 2024 E-Mail:</u> The ellipsis at the end reflects an e-mail system feature to be able to expand out the included copy of the previous rounds of communication or to contract it back to a clickable ellipsis.

<u>Next is Dan Nolan's 3:34 P.M. CST / 4:34 P.M. EST December 23, 2024 response, except for its copy of the previous rounds of the thread:</u>

Dan Nolan   Dec 23, 2024, 3:34PM ☆ ☺ ↩ ⋮
to me ▾

Hi Maurice James Blair,

I apologize for misunderstanding your email. I did read through your previous emails, but my position only allows me to work with Kirkus Indie reviews, so I wanted to confirm with you that we're unable to make changes to the review. Thank you, and I hope you enjoy the holidays!

Best wishes,
Dan Nolan
(he/him/his)
Editorial Assistant of Indie
KIRKUS MEDIA LLC
1140 Broadway, Suite 802
New York, NY 10001

The next few pages show that message together with part of the e-mail's copy of previous rounds.

On Mon, Dec 23, 2024, 3:34 PM Dan Nolan <[redacted]@kirkus.com> wrote:

Hi Maurice James Blair,

I apologize for misunderstanding your email. I did read through your previous emails, but my position only allows me to work with Kirkus Indie reviews, so I wanted to confirm with you that we're unable to make changes to the review. Thank you, and I hope you enjoy the holidays!

Best wishes,
Dan Nolan
(he/him/his)
Editorial Assistant of Indie
KIRKUS MEDIA LLC
1140 Broadway, Suite 802
New York, NY 10001

From: Maurice Blair <[redacted]>
Sent: Monday, December 23, 2024 4:30 PM
To: Dan Nolan <[redacted]@Kirkus.com>
Cc: Ry Pickard <[redacted]@Kirkus.com>; Liza Darnton <[redacted]@gmail.com>; Marcus Padow <[redacted]@fbi.gov>; David Grann <[redacted]>; Steve Raynor <[redacted]@gmail.com>; info@wealthenhancement.com <info@wealthenhancement.com>; Michael Kelsheimer <mkelsheimer@grayreed.com>; dkroll@grayreed.com <dkroll@grayreed.com>; jreed@grayreed.com <jreed@grayreed.com>; Rose Rodriguez <[redacted]>; Johnny Ross <[redacted]>; Ming Blair <[redacted]>; Alex Tse <[redacted]au>; Jennifer Wei <Wei.Excell@gmail.com>; info@harriscountygop.com <info@harriscountygop.com>; hpd.communityaffairs@houstonpolice.org <hpd.communityaffairs@houstonpolice.org>; Jason Peltz <jason.peltz@bartlitbeck.com>
Subject: Re: various

Dan,

Did you bother to read through my correspondence? If you did, then you either forgot that I stated point blank that I am NOT REQUESTING any change to it or you failed to take me at my word!!!!!!!!!!!!!!!!!!!!!!!!!!

If you had responded by stating something like, "We are apprised of the situation. Cheers!" then I would not be hostile. However, your message reflected one of several possibilities: 1) a failure to read through the correspondence, 2) a forgetting a key point of what I stated, or 3) a failure to take me at my word.

To any who encounter this and feel immediate animosity toward me for sending it, bear in mind the message expressed in the last three paragraphs.

Here is a refresher:

"To be clear, I agree with how the recently-published review should stay as-is on account not only to accord with our contractual arrangement but also as a cultural artifact that people can analyze. Online reviews, whether by professionals or amateurs can easily be considered way off base by various authors, publishers, readers, and others, and I actually find your organization's review of *Alternative Beginnings and Endings of All Things*, as off-base as I believe it to be, not as far off-base as I consider your organization's reviews of Clarke & Baxter's *Sunstorm* (2005) and Clarke & Baxter's *Firstborn* (2008)." - M.J.B., December 21, 2024, to Dan Nolan, Ry Pickard, and Stephen Raynor

Had you stated, "We are apprised of the situation. Cheers!" then I would have considered that respectful. I would have almost definitely not even bothered to send any direct response to it.

However, you wrote to me as if presuming disingenuousness, evidently stemming from one of the three possibilities mentioned earlier.

* * *

At this stage I no longer give a damn about if the Democratic Party goes extinct to be replaced by a suitable replacement liberal party much the way that the Republican Party replaced the Whig Party!!!

If I count up all the disrespect toward the bearing of true witness and all the disrespect by the method of the bearing of false witness, even though the Republican Party has not been all that great, the total vitriol either directly or indirectly aimed at me, my family, my religious affiliations, those outside my affiliations yet clearly railroaded, etc., as indicated by personal experience, news, TV, radio, the Internet, etc.. has the full energy associated with the Democratic Party serving as an affront at several times as much as the Republican Party!!!!!!!!!!!!!!!!!!!!!!!!!!!!

Although I cheered for the best in a spirit of agnosticism--whether a Democratic victory in the 2024 general election or a Republican victory in the 2024 general election-- recently, in accordance with the plan mentioned in *Alternative Beginnings and Endings of All Things*, and although I recognize *both the Democratic Party and the Republican Party to be dangerous in their own ways*, also as per what I stated in that book, I decided that the best I could tell from all available information, a Republican victory in that would probably be best. I voted that way, it turned out that way, and I have no regret about it.

To help anyone seeing this understand, here is a simple analogy: You are on a team that has to make one move per round, and you get to vote for what would move your team will make. The team could be analogous to the human race, America, all sentient beings, etc. Therefore, you vote for what you perceive to be best, yet not every single time you vote do you feel anywhere near entirely sure. If you feel uncertain, then you could cheer for the best choice while logically agnostic toward whether your specific vote is on the best side. When I voted I felt quite unsure. Now, the uncertainty is much smaller. I still have a trace of agnosticism toward this, but just in the past few days I have moved very much toward the right, and your choice to write to me in the manner in which you did is the straw that broke the camel-that-held-the-levee-together's back. The levee has broken.

[87]

Now, it is also possible that it might be best for *both the Republican Party and the Democratic Party to go away and get replaced by a new pair of parties*. I do not rule that out in the long run.

I care about soteriology, which I believe a properly functioning First Amendment and a reasonably-liberty-filled U.S. can help very much, yet there are reasons for a degree of skepticism toward both major political parties. That being said, the Republican Party has given my family personally much more reason for confidence than has the Democratic Party. I respect that someone with a very different set of life experiences could think and feel exactly the opposite way. I also covered this in *Alternative Beginnings and Endings of All Things*.

Some, including Marcus Padow, whom I have included with this message may perhaps question and/or condemn that I am revealing one of his FBI email addresses to a bunch of people via this message. However, the patterns of extreme, repeated disrespect from many people and organizations ever since the instant that Steve Estrin threatened that if I were to ever defeat a FinGroup client in serious chess that I would be fired, the patterns of extreme disrespect starting with that very instant have been terrible.

However, the patterns, as viewed holistically, have helped serve enlightenment well, as I have fought back time and time again. Several times I thought, *No need to complain any more about Steve Estrin, Natasha McDaniel, Juan Martinez, Michael Kelsheimer, and all that pattern from before; I've defeated that pattern well enough, and, as the old saying goes, There's no need to beat a dead horse.* However, clearly much of that problem or what emanates from adjacent to that problem persists.

This shall probably be clearer to at least a few of those on this list as there are more forwardings to come.

If Marcus were to attack me for daring to do this, then in the absence of my expressing the following, he might go down the same path he did on a wintry day in the Raleigh-Durham area in the mid-1990s; however, I shall point out differences.

A social member of Psi Upsilon, a woman named Laura Fitzpatrick, was driving a vehicle in which both Marcus and I were passengers. The road was slick due to ice. A wreck ensued. When the police arrived, I briefly cracked a wisecrack joke, thinking it would be funny in the situation. Marcus immediately scolded me, as it was not the correct time for humor. I took that to heart, though I have frequently, nevertheless, been far from perfect since then.

Here is the contrast:

In this case, I am deadly serious. Since I have not encountered any indication from Marcus that I should do anything other than use my own critical thinking, intuition, and such to decide to whom to reveal at least one of his email addresses, and due to the outrageous degree of disrespect that a few segments of American conservatism and many segments of American liberalism have done to me and my family in recent years, I have decided, based on all available factors, that it is best to compose this message exactly as I am composing it and to send it exactly as I am sending it.

[88]

When I composed *Of Dorians, Romans, Hebrews, Whigs. Democrats, Republicans, Indians, and Beyond* (2022, nonprofit/educational booklet, extremely limited distribution; unknown whether any unauthorized modified copies are in circulation besides the authorized unmodified copies; reprinted in 2023 with de minimis authorized modifications), I stopped short of outright stating my thought that it could very well be best for the Democratic Party to go extinct the way the Whig Party did, to be replaced by a better liberal party. However, things changed such that I have now stopped suppressing myself from putting that into writing. That having been stated, I spoke the idea out loud on rare occasions with a few people here and there in portions of late 2021, early 2022, and a few other times, most often by way of saying that it is what Mark R. Levin seems to think best, but that I am not entirely sold on it. However, things have changed. It appears to me at least a 20%–50% probability now.

On the other hand, maybe there are paths forward for the Democratic Party to shape up rather than ship out.

Whatever the case may be, whomever might study the additional forwardings will probably have a better idea. Any of you, even the two on the set of the "to" line and the "cc" line whom I respect the most, viz. Liza Darnton and Marcus Padow, choose to complain to me about how I am conducting this communication, I expect to have no regret about any of it, because the level of insult from various people is such that I am prepared to not even regret this if it were to cause human extinction to happen within 35 seconds after sending it. Actually, let's change that: within one second afterward. See, if anyone with the normal range of capabilities goes toward complaining, compare your plan of complaint or your actual complaint with human extinction within one second after it. When I expressed in many places about "Death before dishonor," I have meant it all the way to every possible instant human extinction. "Life together with honor," that is priceless, but sometimes if one has to go, and a person decides on something being a hill worth dying on, then life can wind up being much more sacrificeable.

Even if you are smug about the idea that it would be impossible, I advise you to let go of your smugness on that and try to understand what I am stating. I genuinely believe in a variety of religious aspects and/or mysterious advanced technological aspects of reality, in large part from utterly surreal experiences, and I am confident that it is very probable that every person will have to in the long run face a situation of nowhere to hide with respect to the totality of their lives relative to whatever the higher power(s) might turn out to be.

When I mentioned repeatedly in *The Science, Religion, Politics, and Cards Trilogy* an absolute commitment to a duty to reality, I meant every word of that.

Regards,
Maurice James Blair

Dan Nolan   Dec 23, 2024, 3:34 PM   ☆   ☺   ↩   ⋮
to me ▾

Hi Maurice James Blair,

I apologize for misunderstanding your email. I did read through your previous emails, but my position only allows me to work with Kirkus Indie reviews, so I wanted to confirm with you that we're unable to make changes to the review. Thank you, and I hope you enjoy the holidays!

Best wishes,

Dan Nolan

(he/him/his)

Editorial Assistant of Indie

KIRKUS MEDIA LLC

1140 Broadway, Suite 802

New York, NY 10001

Next: the Blair response to Nolan's apology for misunderstanding

Maurice Blair <mjblair2956@gmail.com>   Mon, Dec 23, 2024, 4:50 PM   ☆   ☺   ↩   ⋮
to Dan, Ry, Liza, marcus.padow, Rose, Alex, Jason, Michael, Steve ▾

Dan,

Yes, I accept your apology. If you were obligated by policy to answer in one specific way, videlicet the way you answered, then it was one of those square-pegs-versus-round-wholes situations. If that is the case, then I admit that differences of policies cannot fully achieve perfect hybrids of golden rule standards, platinum rule standards, and other such standards, as well as the conscience transcending tangible standards.

Whatever the case may be under the surface, it is good for us to be on good terms with each other now.

An example of something parallel was something I discussed with a coworker circa 2011: most people, as perceived by that then-supervisor, Hong Phan, would evidently prefer moderately sugarcoated statements in the tax services situation that she and I discussed at that time. Not outright distortion, but smoothing sheer dollar cliff effects into a facade of a smooth range, regarding private letter ruling fees if memory serves. I came around to acquiescing to her idea on that, begrudgingly recognizing that although I would in those clients' shoes prefer a complete lack of sugarcoating, most likely majority of clients in that case would prefer sugarcoating.

I strategically did my utmost to decide who would best go onto the cc line and who would best be omitted from the cc line.

Goodwill toward all on here, at least for now, whether you emphasize Happy Holidays, Festivus, Merry Christmas, Happy Hanukah, Season's Greetings, or whatever else!

Kind Regards,

Maurice James Blair

⋯

The next page has a rotated view of an update message, then its copy of the latest of the earlier rounds while omitting its copy of the older installments from the earlier rounds.

[90]

various

Maurice Blair <   >   Wed, Dec 25, 2024 at 7:28 PM
To: Dan Nolan <   @kirkus.com>.   @.fbi.gov, Liza Darnton <
Cc: Ry Pickard <   @kirkus.com>, Rose Rodriguez <   >   .au>, Jason Peltz <jason.peltz@bartlitbeck.com>, Steve
Raynor <   >, Alex Tse <   .au>, Jason Peltz <jason.peltz@bartlitbeck.com>, Steve
<   >, Michael Kelsheimer <mkelsheimer@grayreed.com>, jreed@grayreed.com, Johnny Ross <   >, Ming Blair
Grann <   >, Jennifer Wei <   >, hpd.communityaffairs@houstonpolice.org, info@harriscountygop.com, info@wealthenhancement.com, David
<   >, dkroll@grayreed.com

To Whom It May Concern,

Technical correction regarding the vehicle crash: Memory cleared up enough that I remember now that the wisecrack and the ensuing rebuke were upon first contact between the Chi Delta Chapter of Psi Upsilon-affiliated people with the people who stepped out of the other vehicle, which occurred a while prior to when the police showed up.

Regards,
Maurice James Blair

On Mon, Dec 23, 2024, 4:50 PM Maurice Blair <   > wrote:
Dan,

Yes, I accept your apology. If you were obligated by policy to answer in one specific way, videlicet the way you answered, then it was one of those square-pegs-versus-round-wholes situations. If that is the case, then I admit that differences of policies cannot fully achieve perfect hybrids of golden rule standards, platinum rule standards, and other such standards, as well as the conscience transcending tangible standards.

Whatever the case may be under the surface, it is good for us to be on good terms with each other now.

An example of something parallel was something I discussed with a coworker circa 2011: most people, as perceived by that then-supervisor, Hong Phan, would evidently prefer moderately sugarcoated statements in the tax services situation that she and I discussed at that time. Not outright distortion, but smoothing sheer dollar cliff effects into a facade of a smooth range, regarding private letter ruling fees if memory serves. I came around to acquiescing to her idea on that, begrudgingly recognizing that although I would in those clients' shoes prefer a complete lack of sugarcoating, most likely majority of clients in that case would prefer sugarcoating.

I strategically did my utmost to decide who would best go onto the cc line and who would best be omitted from the cc line.

Goodwill toward all on here, at least for now, whether you emphasize Happy Holidays, Festivus, Merry Christmas, Happy Hanukah, Season's Greetings, or whatever else!

Kind Regards,
Maurice James Blair

A combined transcription of the bodies of those two messages from me:

<u>The 4:50 P.M., December 23, 2024 e-mail to Dan Nolan, cc Ry Pickard, Liza Darnton, Marcus Padow, Rose Rodriguez, Alex Tse, Jason Peltz, Stephen Raynor, and Michael Kelsheimer:</u>

Dan,

Yes, I accept your apology. If you were obligated by policy to answer in one specific way, videlicet the way you answered, then it was one of those square-pegs-versus-round-wholes situations. If that is the case, then I admit that differences of policies cannot fully achieve perfect hybrids of golden rule standards, platinum rule standards, and other such standards, as well as the conscience transcending tangible standards.

Whatever the case may be under the surface, it is good for us to be on good terms with each other now.

An example of something parallel was something I discussed with a coworker circa 2011: most people, as perceived by that then-supervisor, Hong Phan, would evidently prefer moderately sugarcoated statements in the tax services situation that she and I discussed at that time. Not outright distortion, but smoothing sheer dollar cliff effects into a facade of a smooth range, regarding private letter ruling fees if memory serves. I came around to acquiescing to her idea on that, begrudgingly recognizing that although I would in those clients' shoes prefer a complete lack of sugarcoating, most likely majority of clients in that case would prefer sugarcoating.

I strategically did my utmost to decide who would best go onto the cc line and who would best be omitted from the cc line.

Goodwill toward all on here, at least for now, whether you emphasize Happy Holidays, Festivus, Merry Christmas, Happy Hanukah, Season's Greetings, or whatever else!

Kind Regards,

Maurice James Blair

<u>The 7:28 P.M., December 25, 2024 e-mail to Dan Nolan, Liza Darnton, and Marcus Padow; cc Ry Pickard; Rose Rodriguez; Alex Tse; Jason Peltz; Stephen Raynor; Michael Kelsheimer; James L. Reed, Jr.; Johnny Courtland Ross II; Ming Blair; Jennifer Wei; Houston Police Department Community Affairs; Harris County G.O.P.; The Wealth Enhancement Group; David Grann; and Dan Kroll:</u>

To Whom It May Concern,

Technical correction regarding the vehicle crash: Memory cleared up enough that I remember now that the wisecrack and the ensuing rebuke were upon first contact between the Chi Delta Chapter of Psi Upsilon-affiliated people with the people who stepped out of the other vehicle, which occurred a while prior to when the police showed up.

Regards,

Maurice James Blair

Chapter Five: Supplemental Exploratory Screenshots

___An 09:20 Hours & Soon Thereafter 9 JAN 2025 Transitional Note to Preface Screenshots &c.____
Here is a note started about 2 hours 40 minutes before Noon (i.e., at about 9:20 A.M. CST in this case): To clarify the comment on p. 63, first consider this revisitation of a portion of them: "That being said, if someone is so stuck on idea structures of rejecting the very reality of my life itself and the very realities of great ranges of many other people's lives, whether due to bowing down mentally to false absolute mental restrictions of thinking, then that someone is on track to be rebuked by Reality even as measured by that person's own religion(s) and/or science(s) insofar as true at a deep level of reality, for the sentient being in that case is locking into rejecting huge amounts of reality while oblivious to the fact that the sentient being is doing that. Much of this tends to revolve around using identity groups as a crutch with which to think of oneself as somehow inherently owning a total supremacy over anyone lacking that identity group, which can cause the being who fails to grow out of using that crutch to repeatedly turn a blind eye toward individual spiritual and scientific growth while also turning a blind eye toward the value of respecting those who are outside of that person's list of preferred identity groups and yet have, nevertheless paid their dues in terms of achieving individual spiritual and scientific growth."

Several concise examples of how people's own religious and/or scientific practices might hoist them by their own petards are: 1) Jews who lean too heavily on interpreting or allowing rabbis to interpret for them that *Deuteronomy* gives them a greenlight to be extremely harsh on anyone who exhibits strong convictions that superficially seem a logical contradiction to them (i.e., strong convictions that superficially seem to logically contradict the range of simple interpretations of Judaism; of heavily pro-Judaism versions of Christianity, Noahidism, Atheism, and/or Agnosticism; and of other mindsets that tend toward considering Jews and people close to them to have an extreme right to defame the character of anyone—Gentiles, Jews, rich, poor, etc.—whom they believe to be operating contrary to very simple-minded interpretations of a traditional western civilization sensibility that mainly only gives much societal breathing room and living quarters to the range of Judaism, Christianity, Noahidism, Atheism, and Agnosticism, while considering professed belief in Buddhism, Esotericism, Hinduism, Islam, Zoroastrianism, etc. to be prima facie in denial of Reality) may find themselves on the wrong side of how portions of *Leviticus*, especially its expression of divine wrath being a possible consequence that Jews may face if they fail to sufficiently bear true witness, if they bear false witness against neighbors via bearing very harmful false witness against anyone or anything, and/or if they in other ways significantly violate their covenant(s) with G-d. 2) Muslims who lean too heavily on interpreting or allowing imams to interpret for them that *The Qur'an* gives them a greenlight to be extremely harsh on anyone who exhibits strong convictions that superficially seem a logical contradiction to them (i.e., strong convictions that superficially seem to logically contradict the range of simple interpretations of Islam; of heavily pro-Islam versions of People-of-the-Book-ism, Judaism, Noahidism, Christianity, Atheism, and/or Agnosticism; and of other mindsets that tend toward considering Muslims and those close to them to have an extreme right to defame the character of anyone whom they believe to be operating contrary to very simple-minded interpretations of a sufficiently-traditional, sufficiently-Islamic-based Middle-Eastern civilization sensibility that may at times severely restrict societal human breathing room and human living quarters to whatever would conform to the orders of either an imam or a group of imams considered authoritative) may find themselves to have misinterpreted *The Qur'an*. 3) Christians who believe it right for them to persecute others might encounter extreme, biblical, epic rebuke by God/Reality via direct experiences.

Additional concise examples of that are: 4) Science-oriented skeptics who believe it right for them to denigrate, humiliate, and persecute people of faith might encounter extreme, science-fiction-style, epic rebuke by Reality via direct experiences. 5) Buddhists who significantly deviate from something reasonably close to or exactly matching enlightened activity may encounter karma that they will have to overcome by elevating their enlightenment or their proximity to enlightenment. 6) Liberals who fail to sufficiently respect whatever degrees of truth and enlightenment can be real within any portion of conservatism may find that they are neither honoring whatever is true and real about portions of conservatism nor honoring whatever is true and real about portions of liberalism. Therefore, they would need to sink or swim. In other words, they might eventually crises in which failure to make proper changes could be lethal, and, therefore, it would be paramount for them to make the proper changes. 7) Moderates who fail to sufficiently respect whatever happens to be true in liberalism and whatever happens to be true in conservatism may face a day of reckoning or multiple days of reckoning. Adjustments could prove necessary. 8) Conservatives who fail to sufficiently respect whatever degrees of truth and enlightenment can be real within any portion of liberalism may find that they are neither honoring whatever is true and real about portions of liberalism nor honoring whatever is true and real about portions of conservatism. 9) Any hermits and any socialites who insufficiently respect the value of major isolation, the value of major congregation, or both, may have to get back to an openness toward flexible lifestyles that can shift back and forth between isolating to the nth degree and congregating to the nth degree.

_____ An 18:13 Hours & Soon Thereafter 5 JAN 2025 Note_____

A note that started about 6:13 PM U.S. CST 5 January 2025: After having composed the opening and closing statement of this work at about 6 PM U.S. CST 5 January 2025, I embarked at about eighteen past six that evening to look via Metacrawler, Lycos, Bing, and Google web browsers to confirm that components of that statement appear to be absent from the main searchability of the web. I drew that pattern from my heart and mind and soul in contemplating the crux of much of the trouble and travail of all time among human beings and among sentient beings in general. I never witnessed anyone else put that pattern of words or anything anywhere near exactly matching it into print anywhere before I composed it; neither had I heard it anywhere at any time prior to composing it, to the best of the ability of my consciousness to tell from the totality of memory and awareness.

—M. James Blair

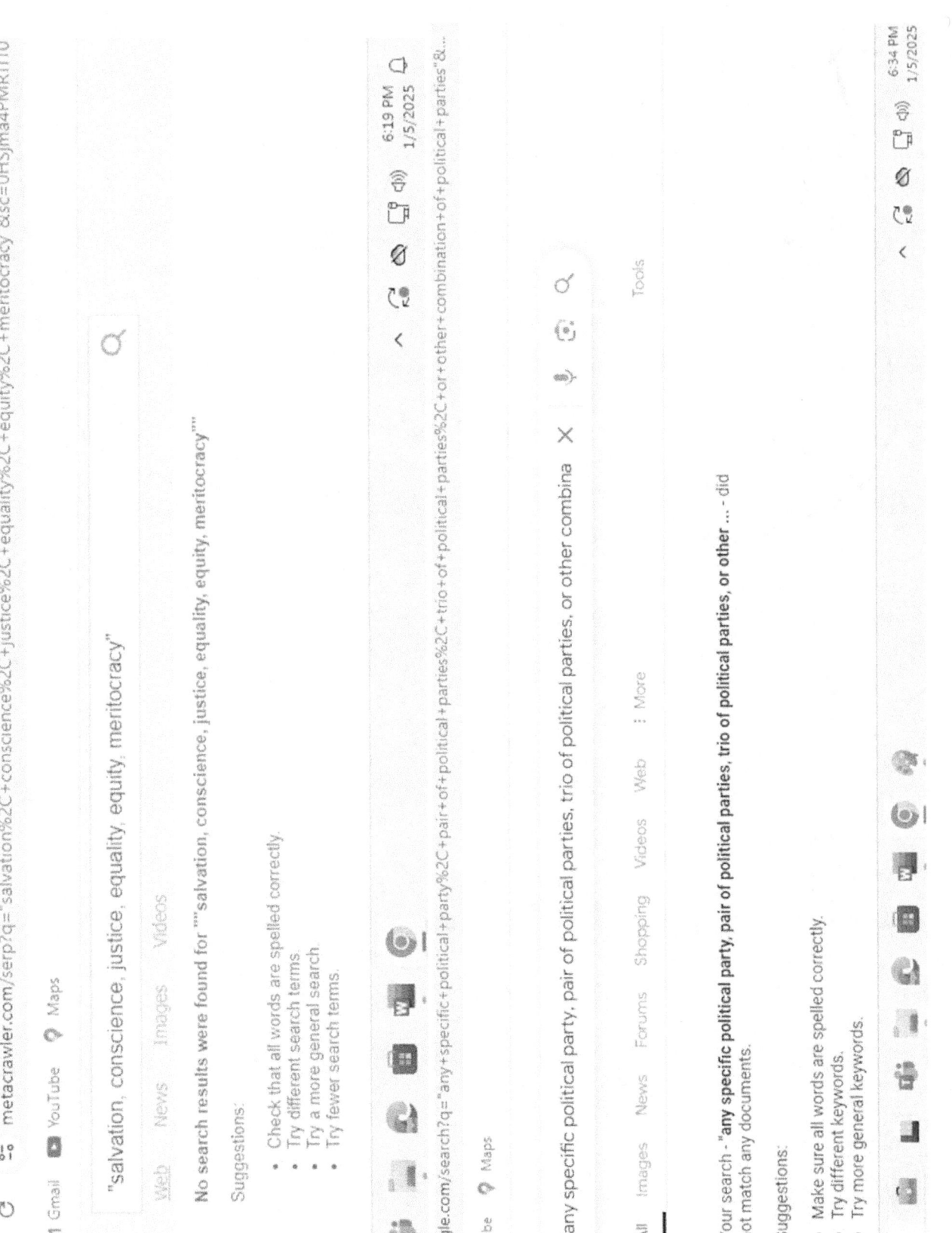

metacrawler.com/serp?q="salvation%2C+conscience%2C+justice%2C+equality%2C+equity%2C+meritocracy"&sc=0HSjma4PMRTi10

M Gmail   ▶ YouTube   ♀ Maps

"salvation, conscience, justice, equality, equity, meritocracy"

Web   News   Images   Videos

No search results were found for ""salvation, conscience, justice, equality, equity, meritocracy""

Suggestions:

- Check that all words are spelled correctly.
- Try different search terms.
- Try a more general search.
- Try fewer search terms.

6:19 PM
1/5/2025

google.com/search?q="any+specific+political+party%2C+pair+of+political+parties%2C+trio+of+political+parties%2C+or+other+combination+of+political+parties"&...

YouTube   ♀ Maps

"any specific political party, pair of political parties, trio of political parties, or other combina   ✕

All   Images   News   Forums   Shopping   Videos   Web   ⋮ More   Tools

Your search - "any specific political party, pair of political parties, trio of political parties, or other ... - did not match any documents.

Suggestions:

- Make sure all words are spelled correctly.
- Try different keywords.
- Try more general keywords.

6:34 PM
1/5/2025

[95]

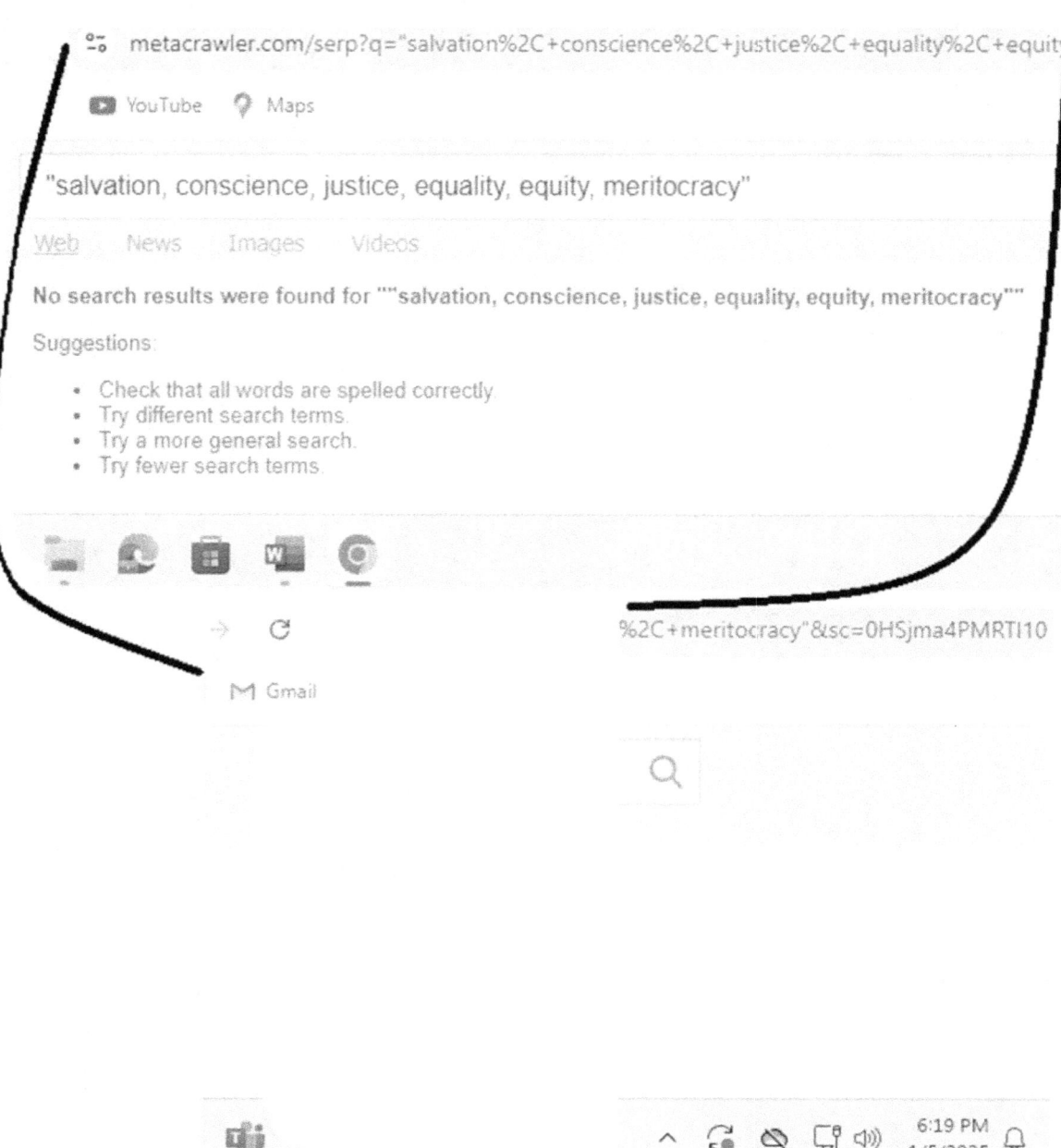

metacrawler.com/serp?q="salvation%2C+conscience%2C+justice%2C+equality%2C+equity

YouTube   Maps

"salvation, conscience, justice, equality, equity, meritocracy"

Web   News   Images   Videos

No search results were found for ""salvation, conscience, justice, equality, equity, meritocracy""

Suggestions:

- Check that all words are spelled correctly
- Try different search terms.
- Try a more general search.
- Try fewer search terms.

→   C

M Gmail

%2C+meritocracy"&sc=0HSjma4PMRTI10

6:19 PM
1/5/2025

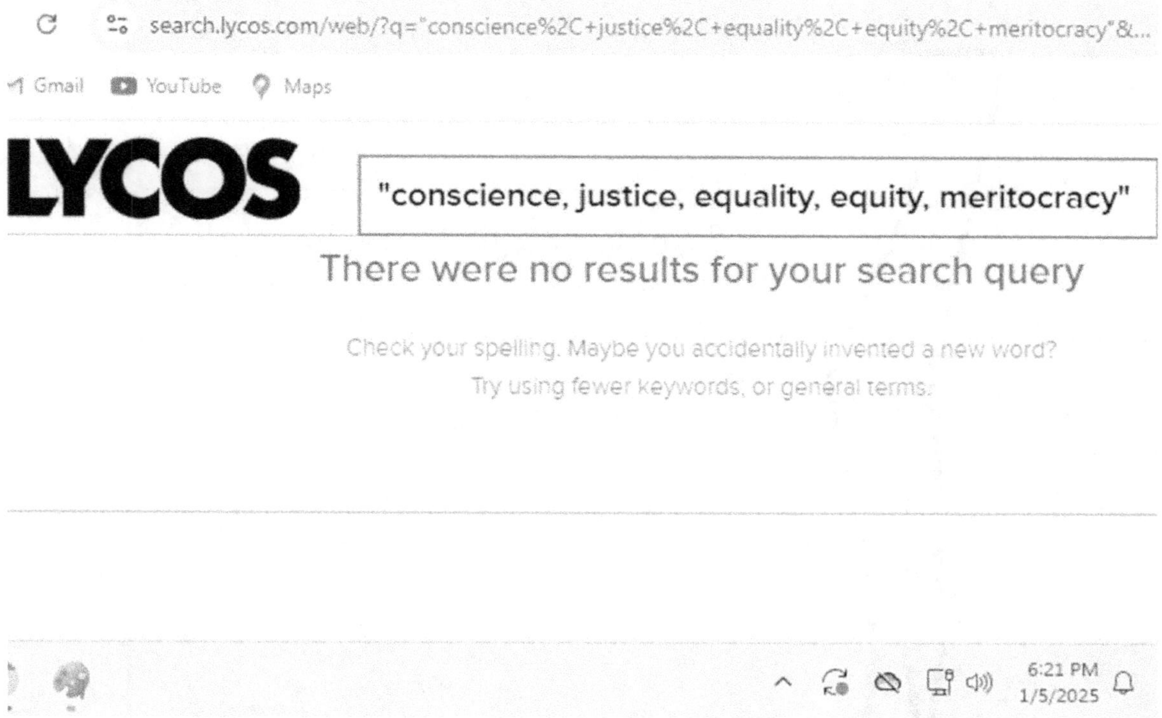
search.lycos.com/web/?q="conscience%2C+justice%2C+equality%2C+equity%2C+meritocracy"&...
Gmail
YouTube
Maps
LYCOS
"conscience, justice, equality, equity, meritocracy"
There were no results for your search query
Check your spelling. Maybe you accidentally invented a new word?
Try using fewer keywords, or general terms.
6:21 PM
1/5/2025

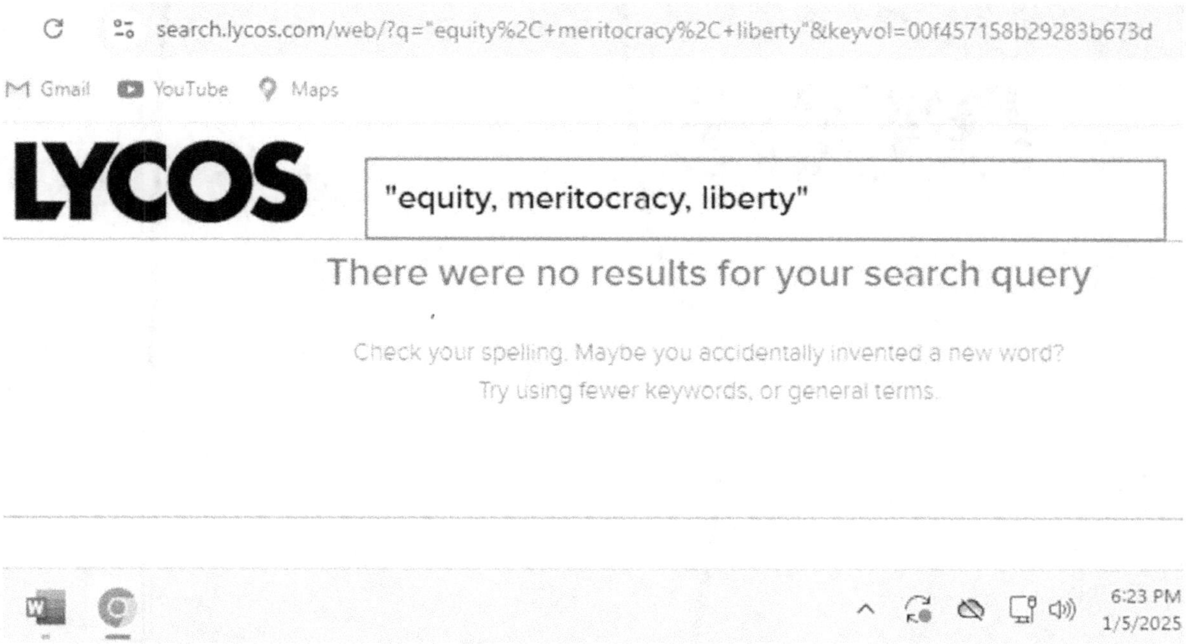
search.lycos.com/web/?q="equity%2C+meritocracy%2C+liberty"&keyvol=00f457158b29283b673d
Gmail
YouTube
Maps
LYCOS
"equity, meritocracy, liberty"
There were no results for your search query
Check your spelling. Maybe you accidentally invented a new word?
Try using fewer keywords, or general terms.
6:23 PM
1/5/2025

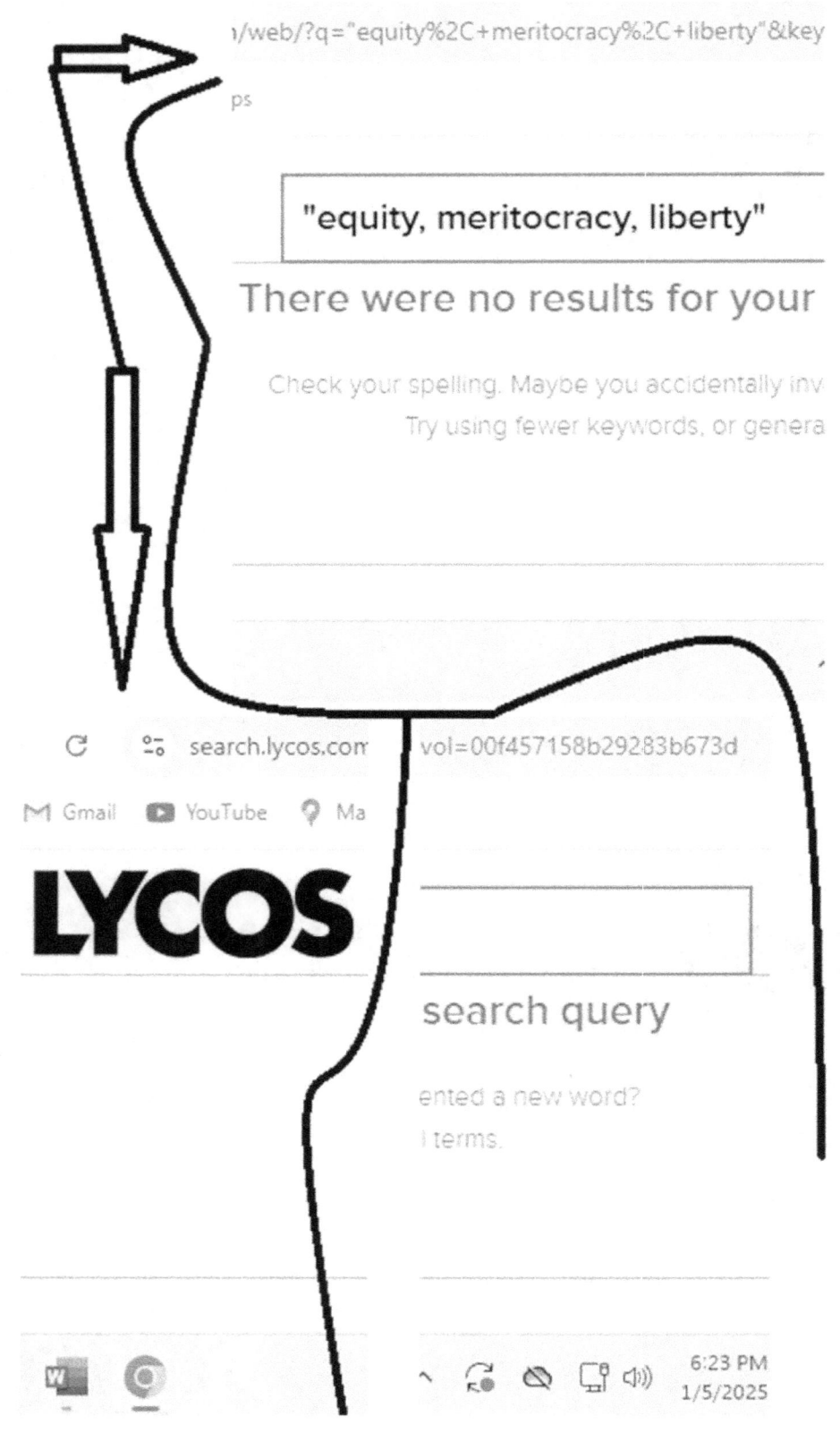

1/web/?q="equity%2C+meritocracy%2C+liberty"&key

ps

"equity, meritocracy, liberty"

There were no results for your

Check your spelling. Maybe you accidentally inv

Try using fewer keywords, or genera

C   search.lycos.com   vol=00f457158b29283b673d

M Gmail   ▶ YouTube   Ma

LYCOS

search query

ented a new word?
l terms.

6:23 PM
1/5/2025

↻ search.lycos.com/web/?q="political+parties+expendable+in+the+long+run"&keyvol=00e604a33...

M Gmail   ▶ YouTube   ♀ Maps

"political parties expendable in the long run"

There were no results for your search query

Check your spelling. Maybe you accidentally invented a new word?
Try using fewer keywords, or general terms.

^ ⊡ ⊘ ⊡ ◁)) 6:25 PM ◻
1/5/2025

---

search.lycos.com/web/?q="combination+of+political+parties+is+expendable"&keyvol=00b8441...

YouTube   ♀ Maps

"combination of political parties is expendable"

There were no results for your search query

Check your spelling. Maybe you accidentally invented a new word?
Try using fewer keywords, or general terms.

^ ⊡ ⊘ ⊡ ◁)) 6:27 PM
1/5/2025

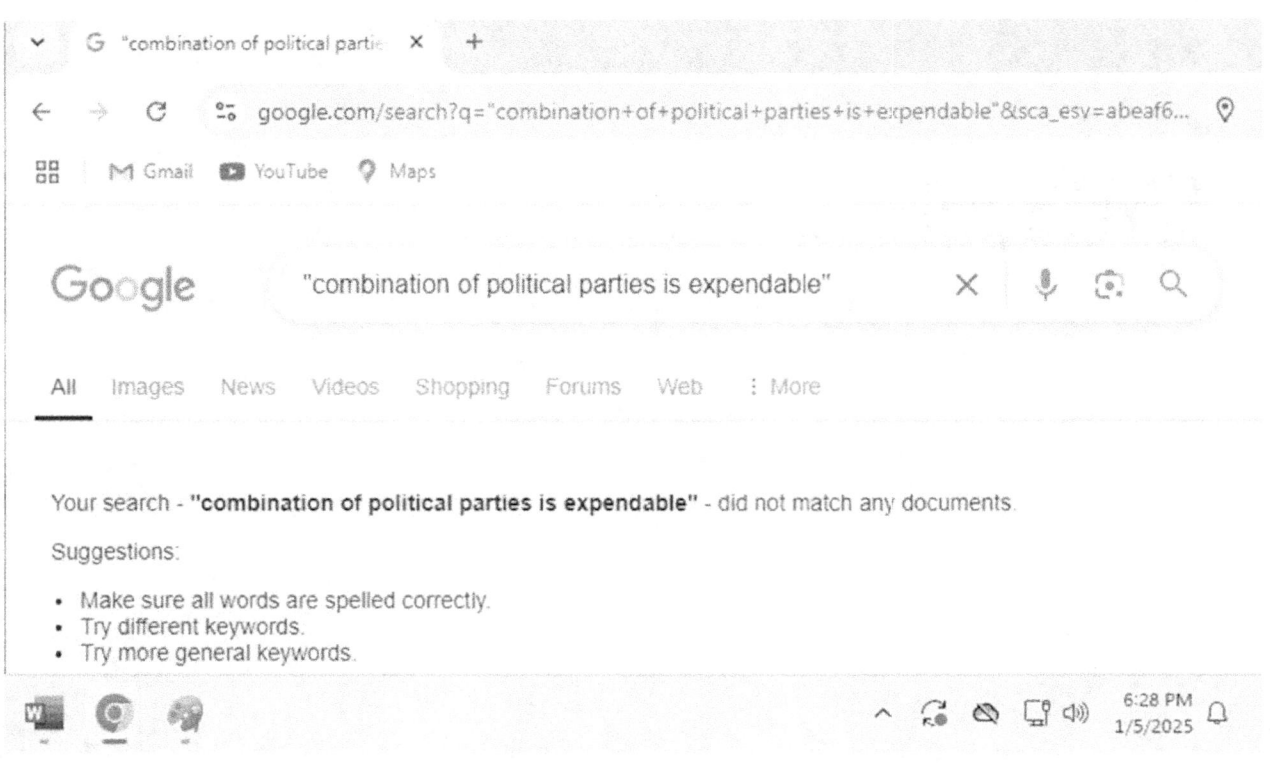

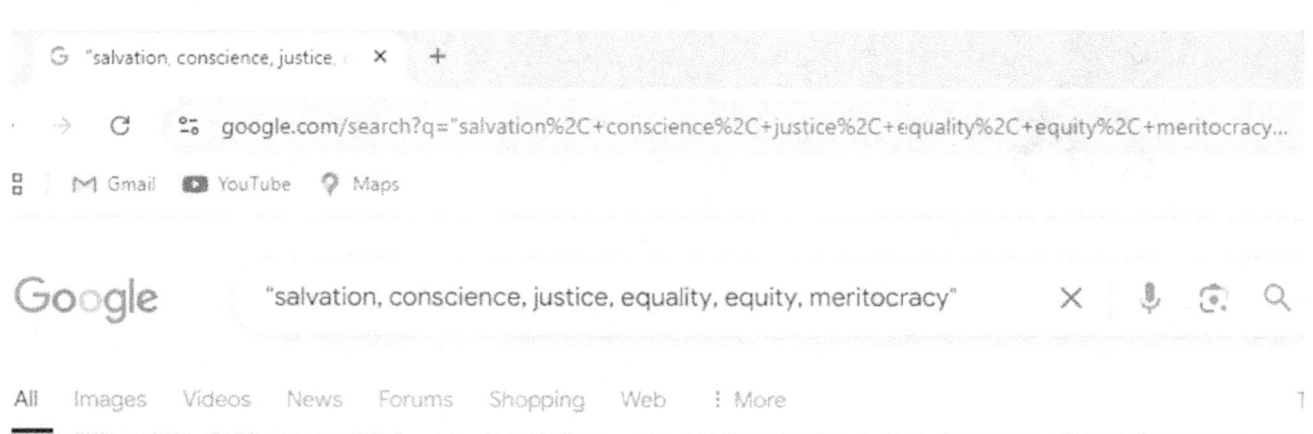

[100]

YouTube   Maps

"salvation, conscience, justice, equality, equity, meritocracy"

Q SEARCH   COPILOT   IMAGES   VIDEOS   MAPS   NEWS   SHOPPING   ⋮ MORE

There are no results for **"salvation, conscience, justice, equality, equity, meritocracy"**

Check your spelling or try different keywords

Ref A: 677b248989714675bb4a96c4477a78d5 Ref B: CHIEEEAP001BD17 Ref C: 2025-01-06T00:32:09Z

6:32 PM
1/5/2025

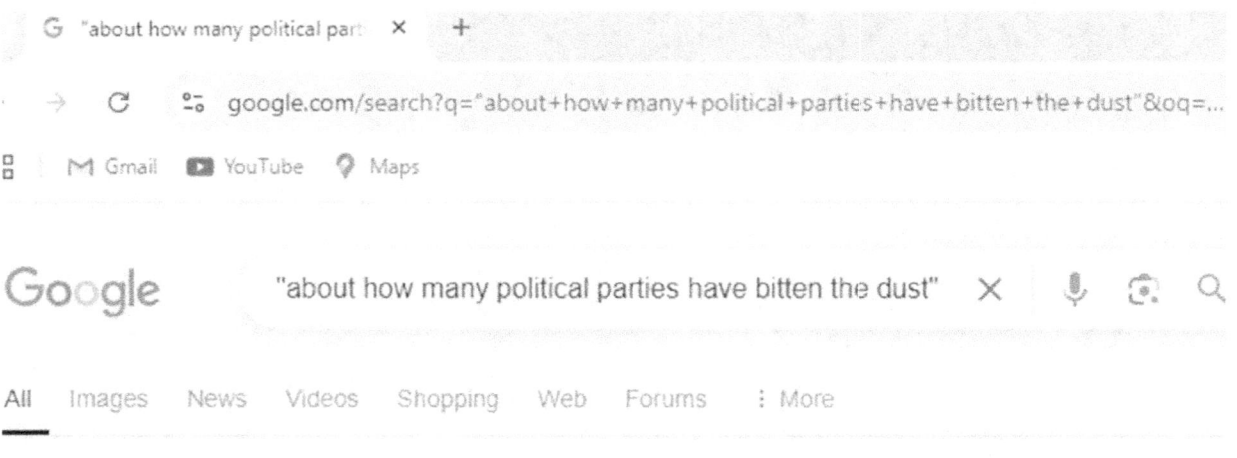

 M Gmail ▶ YouTube 📍 Maps

Your search - **"about how many political parties have bitten the dust"** - did not match any documents.

Suggestions:

- Make sure all words are spelled correctly.
- Try different keywords.
- Try more general keywords.

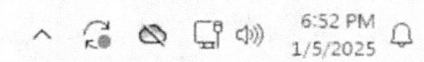 6:52 PM 1/5/2025

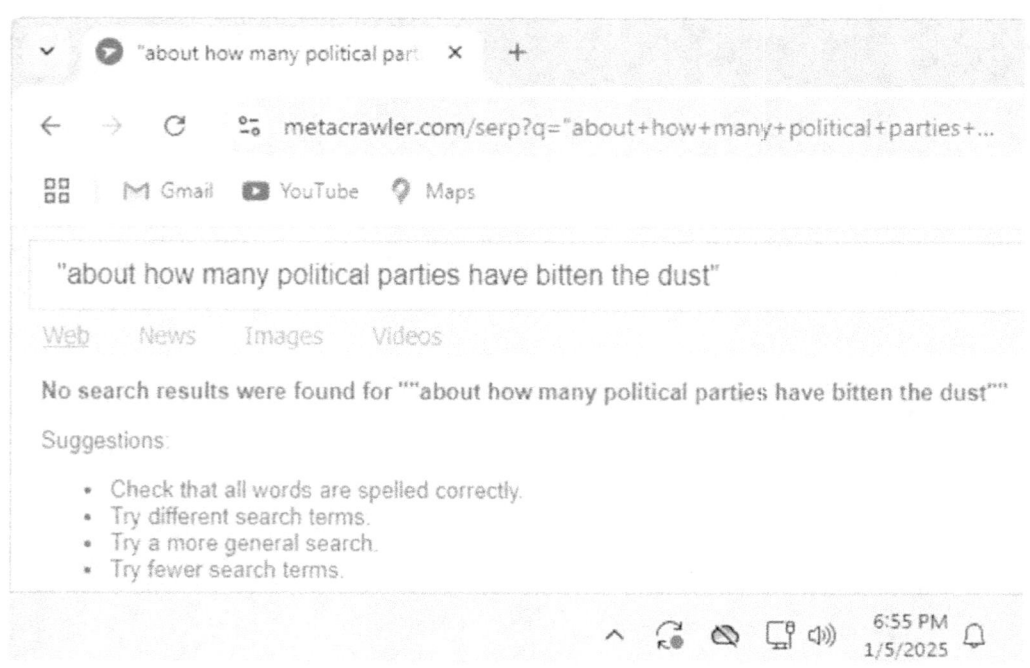

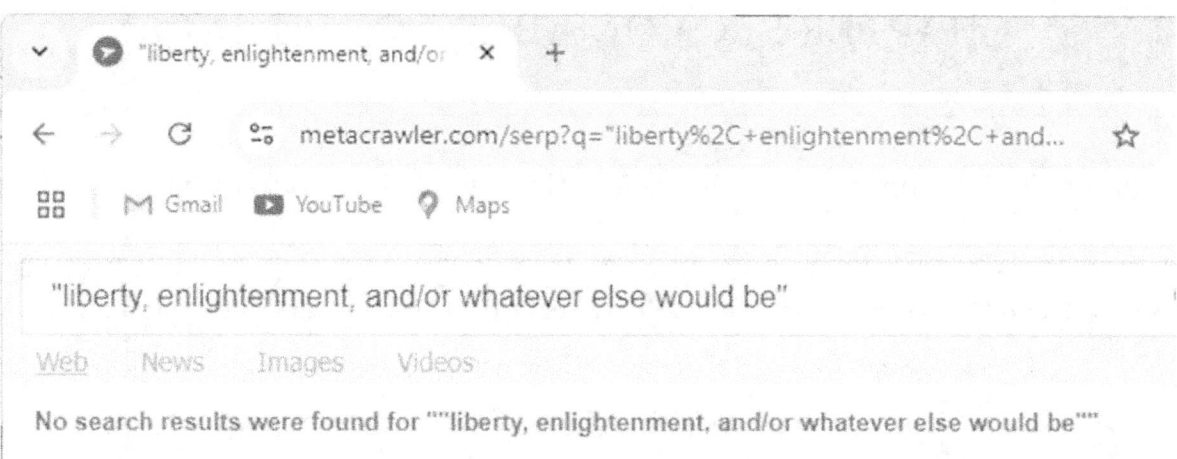

CHAPTER SIX: CONSIDER COMPETING

One Reality. Two Realities. Three Realities. Many Realities. No Realities. All Realities.

Consider Several Competing Idea Structures That Might Have Entered the Public Domain Long Ago:

Common Era = Certified Extinction. Common Era ≠ Certified Extinction.

Points = Points. Points ≠ Points. Joints ≠ Joints. Joints = Joints.

Common Era ≠ Certified Extinction. Common Era = Certified Extinction.

Common Era = Certified Extinction.

Common Era ≠ Certified Extinction.

Consider: Common Era = Certified Extinction. Consider: Common Era ≠ Certified Extinction.

Acid = Acid. Acid ≠ Acid. Acid = Acid.

Base = Base. Base ≠ Base. Base = Base. Base ≠ Base. Base = Base.

Survival = Survival. Survival ≠ Survival. Survival = Survival.

Extinction ≠ Extinction. Extinction = Extinction. Extinction ≠ Extinction.

= = =. = ≠ =. = ≠ =. = = =. = ≠ =.

Freedom is Free. Freedom is Not Free. Freedom is Freedom. Freedom is Not Freedom.

Reality is Reality. One Reality is Not Another Reality. One Reality is Another Reality.

One Reality Transcends Being-Versus-Not-Being Another Reality!!

In 2021, soon after something happened, I posted a photograph from soon after that health crisis for a neighbor who had borrowed my then-residence's phone happened, then, within some moderate amount of time, removed it within that same year. Years later, at 2:43 U.S. CST on December 12, 2024 to be exact, post it again to Facebook, yet, this time, framed with descriptions very differently.

Here is the updated description, which that was part of its mid-December 2024 Facebook post:

"A photograph from after EMS helped a former psychiatrist who had gone into convulsions after screaming at the Social Security Administration. Reportedly, he killed himself about one week later. Cf. a miniature biography of him that appears on pages 89-93 of SCIENCE, RELIGION, POLITICS, AND CARDS (2023). His name was Billy, and to the best of my knowledge, a man named Mario and a man named Justin were the first to walk by and look through a window to see him in a pool of blood in his apartment and to then report it to law enforcement. That Mario was the first to tell me about the death of that Billy, about one day later, and that Justin informed me about three years later that he happened to be next to Mario when they together found the body."

Here, next, is an adjusted-to-grayscale-and-cropped variation of that photograph:

A Lightly-Edited Transcript of Portions of pages 13-15 of *A 24 October 2024 Open Letter to the United States Congress*

<u>Part of a September 10, 2024 message that I, Maurice James Blair, sent to Justin Monroe Haynes, via Facebook Messenger</u>: "'With the advantages also come disadvantages, and, as Lush stated in one of the songs on *Lovelife* (1996): "Life is hard for everyone." Think about it. For example, look at the disasters involving some people with ancestors or other relatives who were in high levels of show business and later found their lives in shambles. Here is a song that we discussed on the phone before about sometime quite a while ago, and which I shall now remind you about, as it relates to that theme of how it is that many people born into wealth and privilege often do not have nearly as great lives under the surface as the poor and underprivileged who may at times feel jealous toward them might imagine: https://www.youtube.com/watch?v=dgMZNJ8VD80 "Richard Cory" by Simon & Garfunkel. Consider that in relation to what I've mentioned to you here.'"

<u>Note</u>: That work is available as a free-distribution in limited quantities paperback and as a free online flipbook. Consider paying a visit to https://mixam.com/share/671b396d0fe21e05bf638a0d if and when feasible. The end of the screenshot on p. 13 of it and the beginning of the screenshot on p. 14 of it in fact duplicated several lines, as mentioned in a follow-up letter. The transcription above adjusted how the source message used the word "tough" where the actual lyric was "hard" in Lush's song "Runaway" on its aforementioned music album.

Now, regarding one of the greatest songs of all time, Procol Harum's "A Whiter Shade of Pale," all sorts of whichever sentient beings are able to understand and feel it might find parallels to all sorts of changes and experiences. Similarly with AC/DC's "Back in Black," which, mysteriously, NASA made sure to use in at least one of its space missions from recent years.

Shifting gears, here's a transcript approximating portions of 2022 to September 2024 conversations between Johnny Courtland Ross II and myself, some cases by phone, other cases in person, an array amalgamated into a semblance of one concise and pithy dialogue:

J.C.R.: You should go to church to try to get a girlfriend, maybe even a wife.

M.J.B.: I only go to churches once in a while in recent decades. Remember, when I worked hard to overcome the entire psychiatric industry and difficulties-of-mind stuff, I found empirically that it has tended to work best for me to primarily identify religiously as a Buddhist most of the time and in most cases. Part of the concern is that, based on experience, many of the women who regularly attend church are of a completely dogmatic mindset of believing that the only right way for anyone to identify in terms of religion is to declare being Christian. I believe in Christianity to some degree much of the time, but I have found what works for me in terms of getting life in general to work well, and the biggest thing in many ways is to be able to stay off of psychiatric medications and to stay away from having to visit psychiatrists for psychiatric services.

J.C.R.: You care more about staying away from the psychiatrists than finding a wife?

M.J.B.: Yes. That is, staying away from the patient-doctor relationship as a psychiatric patient. If I informally meet a few psychiatrists here and there devoid of that, then that could be fine.

J.C.R.: You've got it all figured out, do you?

M.J.B.: In many ways, none of us has it all figured out. That reminds me of an idea many self-help experts, many musicians, and others have expressed: We should all be ready to learn new stuff.

J.C.R.: I went to Methodist churches before, and I never felt like they were trying to force dogmas over on people much at all.

M.J.B.: You mean they were largely telling people that they should believe in Jesus Christ, but they could work out many of the other details themselves, finding what works for them. Is that your experience of that?

J.C.R.: Yes. It's sort of the opposite of that problem I had with the Mormon lady I dated in college. With her, it later turned out that the Mormon Church would try to tell Mormon couples how to run their lives, what to do, where to go, and that's why I broke up with her.

M.J.B.: Yes, you told me about that before. That being said, I remember hearing from some of them that they prefer to be called members of The Church of Jesus Christ of Latter-Day Saints, rather than being called Mormons.

J.C.R.: That's quite a mouthful!

M.J.B.: Yes, but then they also have the approved nickname, LDS.

J.C.R.: You wouldn't have to go Methodist. What about other sects, is there a Christian church where you might consider getting involved and finding a bride?

M.J.B.: Actually, the one mainstream Christian church that I might consider seriously getting thoroughly involved with in a way comfortable might be the Christian Scientists, more formally known as members of The Church of Jesus Christ, Scientist.

J.C.R.: Dear God! If you do that, I'll see you at your funeral.

M.J.B.: Oh, please?! You're complaining again about the idea that their followers can tend to go overboard with avoiding traditional medical treatment. That's what you're getting at, isn't it?

J.C.R.: Yes. I'm telling you, that's a problem. They're a cult!

M.J.B.: Look, I actually respect them very highly. Now, of course, sometimes people should use some of the traditional western medicine. However, the drug companies and a bunch of the doctors have been overprescribing people tremendously.

J.C.R.: You do have a point there. Think about it, though. I'm thinking you could get involved with a more normal sect of Christianity.

M.J.B.: There's the old saying, "The proof is in the pudding." You know, I've told it to you before, and I'll say it again right now: I found much of what would work for me to avoid getting involved with the terrible mental difficulties from before, and I found much of what works for me to continue staying a former psychiatric patient instead of being a psychiatric patient. Buddhism is a big part of that, and therefore, no matter how much someone might believe dogmatically in reasons to avoid paying any respect to it, I respect it due to having experienced proof of at least a major degree of truth in much of it. This is not to say that I believe that everyone has to completely convert to Buddhism in the long run, but anyone who walks contrary to whatever is really true within Buddhism or anyone or anything else or whatever is trying to fight with Reality Itself.

J.C.R.: So you think you have it all figured out, do you?

M.J.B.: As I said before, I have much of it figured out, but there's still lots of stuff I haven't figured out. I continue to adapt.

J.C.R.: Just stay away from getting very involved with the Scientologists. They'll take all your money.

M.J.B.: You're being paranoid about them. Or, should I say, *us*, because I officially joined them about three-fourths of the way into the year 2023. Look, I am reasonably cautious about paying money to the Church of Scientology.

J.C.R.: Good, because many people go broke spending money on them.

M.J.B.: Look, there's a way that I can explain much of this. Consider an analogy: People getting involved with different religious organizations and religions is very much like how people manage their diets. Some people can maybe maintain great health by eating almost all their food from one fast food restaurant chain, yet other people need more diversity in their diet. Also, if people get way too involved with anything for their own good, then it could be bad. Maybe some people reach deep involvement with Scientology or LDS or Christian Science or whatever and it goes very well for them. Maybe in their case, it is exactly what is best for their niche within Reality. Other people, though, could get heavily involved with some religious organization and find that it is like overly tilting their entire diet into being too narrow and not actually adapted well for whatever genetic and lifestyle factors they face. However, in my case, I have arrived at a well-diversified set of changing involvement and beliefs with many different religions and many different religious organizations. It is not like how some people get all wrapped up into one religious organization such that having problems with that one can bring down almost everything in their lives. Others get all wrapped up into one religious organization and it goes well for them. Then there are people who seem to be doing well without much, if any, organizational involvement. "Different strokes for different folks," as the old saying goes. Speaking of that, do you remember watching the TV show *Diff'rent Strokes*?

J.C.R.: I saw some of that. Didn't all the main actors in it get into trouble in real life?

M.J.B.: Everyone gets into trouble in real life, but I think you're talking about getting into more trouble than most people get into. I think at least two or three of the actors got into much more trouble than most people, and there was some serious tragedy. That reminds me of that mystery involving the death of Bob Crane.

J.C.R.: Oh yeah, we've discussed this before. He died in some sort of S&M act or something like that, didn't he?

M.J.B.: I kind of remember seeing part of a documentary about his life. Yes, it was either that he died in connection with a kinky, S&M act or someone might have staged it to look like he died that way.

J.C.R.: There's something else I want to ask your opinion on: What do you think happens to us when we die?

M.J.B.: I don't entirely know, and maybe none of us among the living knows for sure. There is, though, a way of experientially proving something like a microscopic trace of all the different theories of what happens. I kind of experienced that in 2007.

J.C.R.: Interesting, but I'm not sure if I understand what you're saying.

M.J.B.: It's a sort of thing that people would have to experience directly to understand. With words I could only get you so far; to really understand it, you would have to directly arrive there at that awareness. Something else about this is that even with that microscopic provability of at least a trace of a multilayered reality, it still leaves a gargantuan unknown. The main bulk of the reality of what happens after we die is still something that seems to me completely unknown, and I continue to be uncertain whether we ever wind up knowing for sure about it.

A cropped-on-8-January-2024-and-adjusted-to-grayscale version of a photograph that I took on November 2, 2023 at 9:12 P.M. in Harris County, TX; I posted the color, full-size version to Facebook 4:45 P.M. on December 13, 2024, visible at https://www.facebook.com/photo/?fbid=10213417821235684&set=pcb.10213417821555692 :

<u>Regarding the photo on the previous page, I combined the following explanation with the in-color, full version of it when posting it to Facebook:</u> I took this photograph on November 2, 2023 after helping a man named John Ross (not to be confused with the arctic explorer John Ross (1777-1852)) move a bunch of his books from one storage unit to another and to donate many of his books to charity. About two days prior I had mentioned to him how Garry Kasparov had stated in portions of 2015 to early 2016 a preference for Marco Rubio to become president, yet Senator Rubio had been too rigid and insufficiently extemporaneous with crafting words to point from different angles when Governor Christie was labeling him "a bubble boy" and then doubling down on saying that the rigidity of repetition of talking points without thinking on his feet to say things in a new set of his own words "proved" Sen. Rubio to "be a bubble boy," and, seemingly oblivious, Sen. Rubio again stuck to identical or nearly identical scripted "talking-points-style" words. Also, I had mentioned to him something like, "What if Rubio had been able to think on his feet enough to not fall into Christie's trap and had, furthermore, fired at Trump the shot of saying, 'Look, he can't stay inside the box to save his life.' What then? Who knows whether or not that would have changed the course of history very much?" BTW, President Trump has seemed to at least sometimes in 2024 get better at being able to think and act inside the box when called for it. On another note, part of the reason I posted the Zager & Evans song "Fred" after my mother fell down, became badly injured, went into a hospital, and got out, wearing a cast, was that there was a parallel in which, though sometimes having been a friend of the family, he partway offended me and greatly offended my mother early in my mother's recovery process. That was by jokingly mentioning to me an idea that he might wish me to consider sometime building a storm cellar in the backyard and intentionally locking my mother in that cellar without her consent, then letting her out after imprisoning her there for two days straight, expecting her to behave in a way more manageable for society. Not long after that, I chose to inform my mother of his crude joke of that idea. Not long after that, there was a call in which John and I spoke with each other, then my mother spoke with him briefly. Suddenly, she angrily threatened him over the phone, and he has gone silent toward my family since then. I have no regrets on this, for a long time I worked hard to honor his request to decline to name him in any of my books, yet once he went silent after that strange conflict, I decided, you know what, he had already belittled many of what I considered among the best things I had accomplished in this life, therefore, I would no longer give a damn about how he told me that if I would ever name him directly in a book, then that would amount to the end of his friendship with me; I decided to unilaterally declare to two people by e-mail that the friendship between me and that Johnny Ross II was over, and that whether he would try to reconcile with me later or not, I would choose to have no inhibition any longer from sooner or later naming him directly in a book. That was because he had shown himself time and time again to be among the 99.5% or so of people who are a huge part of the problem with the human race, and it was only the moderate degree of friendship and his imposition that had held me back from directly naming him, and things had changed. Eventually, I decided that I would directly identify him via the free booklet and ebooklet A 24 OCTOBER 2024 OPEN LETTER TO THE UNITED STATES CONGRESS, a work with which I alpha-and-omega bombed a huge amount of what was wrong with each and every political party and each and every sentient being.

<u>Here is a copy of the main text I placed in the 10/15/25 song post referenced in the photo explanation copy:</u>
Here is a song that has probably seldom, if ever, been used as part of introduction to a political campaign speech: https://www.youtube.com/watch?v=aLO-EG90J9M

Here is something that I posted to Facebook on October 18, 2024 from Houston, Texas: After hesitancy to mention this, here goes: After watching multiple CHILDREN OF THE CORN movies in 2021-2023, I finally read "Children of the Corn" by Stephen King in mid-to-late August 2024.

Posted to https://www.facebook.com/mjblair on October 21, 2024 from the city of Houston in the state of Texas was this: Clarke & Kubrick probably made the best decision to sidestep the earlier idea of adapting that and instead generating 2001: A SPACE ODYSSEY, and Syfy probably made the best decision to adapt that decades later. https://www.youtube.com/watch?v=iR3cYGMY7Zk

Also posted there that day from that city was: https://www.youtube.com/watch?v=SfPSCDu6NQ4 . "Bob Dylan's 115th Dream" seems less like a dreamscape and more like regular life in recent years.

The next day, which was the 22nd, I posted to that platform: "As I have mentioned to multiple people in recent years, some directly by spoken word, others indirectly by presenting books that point toward it, _____." Imagine anyone stating that and variations of what to fill into the blank.

Also on 22 OCT 2024, I posted to Facebook: Some consider "DDD patterns" in connection with "digital-digital-digital" works; others consider "DDD patterns" in connection with "idiocy-idiocy-idiocy" works. Consider your reactions--whether involving "wisdom-wisdom-wisdom" works or otherwise--to the following video: https://www.youtube.com/watch?v=cUXrEhE4DHs

Another M.J.B. October 22, 2024 C.E. Facebook post: Here is a video that can compare and contrast with much of television and the Internet: https://www.youtube.com/watch?v=mbzWWmf9oj0

Notice that the second, third, fifth, and sixth items above included hyperlinks. If we use 2, 5, and 6 to label them for the sake of efficiency and make official reference markers to go with them, then this is what we get:

2. "Childhood's End (Syfy) Official Trailer [HD]" as posted by YouTube account "televisionpromosdb" circa 2016.

3. "Bob Dylan's 115th Dream" as posted by Bob Dylan's YouTube account circa 2016.

5. "'Carlos Mencia A Bit of Mencia "Dee Dee Dee's and the news"'" as posted by Carlos Mencia's YouTube account circa 2019.

6. "Jordan Peterson: The Power of Gossip and the Cost of Reputation Damage" as posted by YouTube account "litlmike" circa 2024.

---

* * * * *

A October 26, 2024 Facebook post via a Houston computer: Here is the Saturday Night Live sketch that I briefly mentioned in the 22 February 2024 phone call that The Michael Berry Show publicly broadcasted on 15 March 2024 and 05 July 2024: https://www.youtube.com/watch?v=4vX5OEUt4ZU Note: The link I included with that was to Saturday Night Live's YouTube account's "Adults Living at Home - Saturday Night Live" video.

Although I am very capable of structuring online communications in very linear, western-civilization-conformist-style ways, I often intentionally decline to do that. One of the factors weighing on me in the direction toward more of a nonlinear, eastern-civilization-inscrutable-sage-style way is to defend myself from risks of extreme mental difficulties, in that experience has demonstrated time and time again in my life that a heavy dose of the western, extremely-linearly-arranged thought patterns tends to arrive at the realities of stuff like Charlie Munger's warnings about academia and ordinary-range business practices often succumbing to focusing too much on what a given model says, ignoring the various second-order, third-order, fourth-order, and greater chain-reaction effects, due to people over-simplifying and then turning a blind eye to the more complete reality.

Behold a copy of what I posted to https://www.facebook.com/mjblair while in Houston on November 21, 2024: As part of taking a Dr. Eric Durham speech class in mid-2009, I silently thought, "Yes, I can dumb down my writing to the one-thesis-support-conclusion academic convention, and when I get back into the regular real world outside I can go back to hermetically sealing great portions of writings from the intangible levels of Tsogyal-style, Tolkien-style, and Munger-style attacks on excessively-linear and excessively-unified writing." I have known full well since he clarified for me that the multipronged Zen transcendence approach to writing was not what the academic paper-writing for the purpose of his scoring would be built around, and I adjusted accordingly. However, back into the real world, I know from having directly experienced things way beyond the ordinary, that in general, in many cases I should aim to design writings with THE ABSOLUTE REALITY / GOD / ADIBUDDHA / ADIDHARMA / THE ENTIRE RETINUE OF THE MAIN BUDDHAS, BODHISATTVAS, AND DHARMA PROTECTORS - those beyond the regular stage of our universe's reality - as the primary audience, with the fellow, regular humans - who are in some sense also of a cast that can encounter all manner of special effects from those who are in some way beyond and somehow at times loosely scripting and tightly directing much of the action - mainly as secondary audience. Similarly, with all actions.

*   *   *   *   *

*   *   *   *   *

*   *   *   *   *

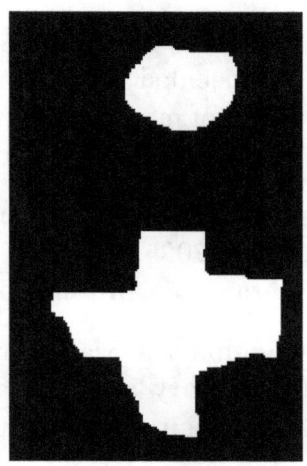

*   *   *   *   *

*   *   *   *   *

*   *   *   *   *

<u>A Summary of A Few January Seventh-to-Eighth, Twenty-Twenty-Five Communications</u>

At about 8:30 A.M. U.S. CST, I posted to my friend Armando Martinez's Facebook profile, "Happy Birthday! Too bad some of the women I dated last year were, one after another, not into the blood-and-guts-and-mayhem movies, but it is good some platonic friends are into them. I'm only into them some of the time, but I really love them when I get around to them, and I can't help but wonder if it's kind of like a woman not feeling comfortable with the entire horror genre will steer her away from my entire family with its intensity, but, hey, with or without more dating, I've got at least a few platonic friends like you who are favorable toward horror movies and reasonably favorable toward the intensity that my family, including myself, bring to this multiverse. Happy Birthday! Also, thanks again for discussing some horror and science fiction and politics in what I consider a reasonably-balanced way in many cases in the recent years, thanks Armando, have a great day!"

(His profile on that is at https://www.facebook.com/profile.php?id=100014670691265 as of the second day after the U.S. Congress certified that President Trump won his third U.S. Presidential attempt, after having won one out of two attempts previously.)

Very early in the day, in fact within minutes of starting to use the Internet a while after dawn, I noticed articles mentioning that Meta had decided to make a major change, one that I first heard about a little earlier in the post-dawn portion of morning. Here is an identification list of a sample of articles mentioning this, with references to each as accessed on the day[*] after they reached the public:

• Duffy, Clare. "Meta is getting rid of fact checkers. Zuckerberg acknowledged more harmful content will appear on the platforms now." January 7, 2025. CNN.
   https://www.cnn.com/2025/01/07/tech/meta-censorship-moderation/index.html

• Paul, Katie; Mukherjee, Supantha; and Sophia, Deborah Mary. "Meta shelves fact-checking in policy reversal ahead of Trump administration." January 7, 2025. Reuters.
   https://www.reuters.com/technology/meta-ends-third-party-fact-checking-program-adopts-x-like-community-notes-model-2025-01-07/

• Zuckerberg, Mark. "It's time to get back to our roots around free expression. We're replacing fact checkers with Community Notes, simplifying our policies and focusing on reducing mistakes. Looking forward to this next chapter." January 7, 2025. Facebook.
   https://www.facebook.com/zuck/videos/1525382954801931

"Fact checkers have been too politically biased and have destroyed more trust than they've created."
—Meta CEO Mark Zuckerberg; Tuesday, January 7, 2025

"What started as a movement to be more inclusive has increasingly been used to shut down opinions and shut out people with different ideas, and it's gone too far."
—Meta CEO Mark Zuckerberg; Tuesday, January 7, 2025

---

[*] The day mentioned in the underlined title near the top of this page is what the R.O.C. calendar counts as January 8, 114, whereas the Gregorian Calendar counts as January 8, 2025. As is a convention in the publishing industry as conducted in North America in recent centuries, year number references in this book when not otherwise stated in this are as measured by the Gregorian Calendar.

"It feels surreal that about four minutes before this post I visited Mark Zuckerberg's Facebook page, and to the best of my memory, it was the first time I've ever visited his Facebook page. (Sans tagging pages, occurrence of this post: ~10:12 A.M. CST, 8 JAN 2025.)"

A related thought is that one of the first few things I did when I joined X on April 1, 2024 was to visit Elon Musk's official X page, whereas I had either almost never or actually never visited Mark Zuckerberg's Facebook page from the time of joining Facebook in mid-2009 until about 10:08 A.M. U.S. CST on January 8, 2025.

Here's another thought: When we age and have more experiences under our belts, some old artifacts can take expanded or altered meanings. For example, we can revisit the motion picture film *Stalag 17* (1952), audiovisuals featuring R. Lee Ermey (1944-2018), and diverse items demonstrating some of the activities of Rogers Hornsby (1896-1963), including his sports performance records.

Similarly, we can contemplate the literary, sports, scientific, and other activities of all sorts of our fellow sentient beings, be they of any gender, age, accomplishments, fame, infamy, notoriety, scandal, acclaim, honor, and/or whatever else.

A statement that probably first became uttered out loud on Earth sometime in the third quarter of the second millennium C.E. (also called by some the second millennium A.D.) or earlier, in one language or another or in multiple languages by separate, independent creation or whatever, and, which is, therefore, probably in the public domain, though I have no conscious recollection of having heard or seen it expressed before composing it here on January 8, 2025 to be part of this paragraph, is as follows: "Reality can seem very real, and reality is sometimes super surreal." —Unknown, circa the period from one 1750 to the other 1750 (as per this hypothesis).

Of course, it may well be unknown to all or nearly all living beings how many instances, if any, of the uttering of that statement and/or the writing of that statement occurred in the 3,500-year period estimated for when the hypothesis posits it to have most likely first happened on Planet Earth. This also points out another facet: Why be so narrow-minded as to be extremely Earth-centric? If there really are multitudes of intelligent species spread out over the universe, and many times as many spread out over the multiverse, as some of the scientifically-minded have conjectured, then almost everything that any earthling has ever received credit for discovering or creating as a quote or a meme or whatever could very well have already been discovered and/or created in another solar system somewhere, a while prior to when any given earthling—credited or otherwise—created or discovered it. "C.E." could be thought of as an abbreviation for lots of different stuff; for example, Constellational Extraterrestrials, Ceteris Erotis, Cover Entirely, Creole Enchantment, Crocodilian Exhilaration, Compassionate English, Confounded English, Chinese English, Crucified Ecuadorian, Canadian Ecuadorian, Canned Eccentricity, Cetera Et, Corpus Et, Carmenta Et, and Combined Encampment.

Yet another thought is a hypothesis, based on the sum total of everything up to the time of stating this, that recalcitrance by many liberals is one of the biggest problems that the Democratic Party faces, that premature apprehension is one of the biggest problems that the Republican Party faces, and that excessive extremism and excessive polarization are problems almost everybody faces.

"A Brief Train of Thought That Travels Smoothly to Arrive at Its Destination"

After composing and editing the previous page several times, I started to worry. I had thumbed through *The New Collegiate Latin & English Dictionary* (Traupman, John C., 1966; Bantam) in order to help come up with a reasonably suitable candidate for which version of Erotic, Erotica, Eros, et cetera to use, eventually using the Latin phrase "Ceteris Erotis" as a best attempt of taking the frequent "Ceteris Paribus" and making it into something more erotic. At first, I felt fine about the decision, but worry started to sink in about it, thinking along the lines of, *What if some group out there already has that as a motto? If I do this kind of randomly, then some readers could lump me together with such a group, even though I may have essentially nothing to do with it. Hm, I better take a look around the Internet to get a better idea of whether or not to include that phrase in this book.*

Next, I performed a couple of searches on Metacrawler. Here is a screenshot of some of what happened to show on the monitor upon conducting the second attempt:

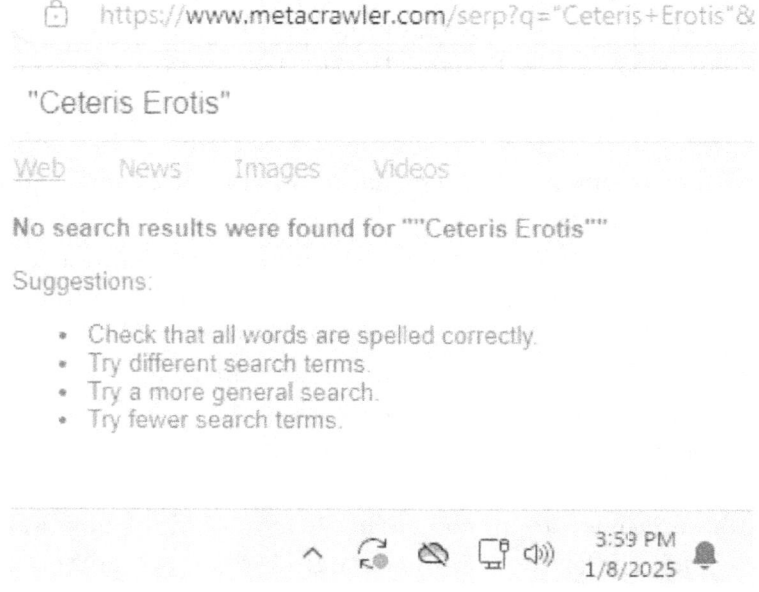

The string of characters that the search produced for its resultant URL:
https://www.metacrawler.com/serp?q=%22Ceteris+Erotis%22&sc=h1qZk7rA9ggB10

Combine this with whatever else we—the publisher and the author—consciously know about, and here is where that thought train arrives: Therefore, to the best of the author's knowledge and the publisher's knowledge as of the time of going to print with this book, either a) there is no organization strongly considered by pop culture, academia, et cetera, as heavily associated with the phrase "Ceteris Erotis" or b) any organization(s) associated with it are currently profoundly obscure.

<u>Analysis of Several Outtake Ideas and Presentation of More Gateways</u>

During portions of January 9, 2025, I considered arranging some later stages of the book to reflect a table of contents that would include something along the lines of:

However, I decided instead to go with the following pattern:

- Adding "Analysis of Several Outtake Ideas and Presentation of More Gateways" on pages 117-118.

- Creating a brief, flash fiction story to complete this chapter.

"An Occurrence at the Northeast Corner of Clarke and Preston"

by M. James Blair

(Preface: The characters of this story are either fictitious or used fictitiously. Perhaps this very conversation has occurred in history on at least one occasion, independently created by some whom the author of this story never witnessed prior to composing it. The author's composition of it is straight from his mind, his ability to tune in to Reality in general, and various of the patterns in and adjacent to whatever and whatever else. Therefore, although similarities are coincidental, for all the author knows at the time of composing it, a little past Noon Central Standard Time as experienced in U.S. zip code 77063 on the 9th Day of January 2025 either C.E. or A.D. as considered by reference to the Gregorian Calendar, it just might be possible that in some actual reality somewhere it exactly occurred as part of real-life phenomena. The author shall now dedicate this to memory of how a woman named Ana Akunde told him nearly two decades prior to say out loud the number pattern 3, 6, 9, 12, and, after hearing her say that, he said out loud to her, "3, 6, 9, 12." Upon further reflection, Ana Akunde proved in the long run as perfect in her brief interaction with the author for the author's healing as Liza Darnton proved over a span of about three decades, all things considered up to the time of composing this short story. That being said, the author plans to include that Liza in his last will and testament, if he bothers to ever make an official last will and testament someday instead of merely making unofficial drafts for what it might event- ually become. In many senses every situation is unique, and the author believes he might best honor that Liza by including her in his official last will and testament if there ever is one someday, whereas he believes one of the best ways to honor that Ana is by omitting any direct reference to her in his official last will and testament if he ever finalizes such a last will and testament someday. Now, without further ado, here is that tale.)

Lucy and Arthur wondered how many other Lucies and Arthurs there might be in the cosmos.

They also wondered if they lived in a universe that was part of a multiverse. At some stage the both of them had watched the first episode of the second season of the TV show *Kids in the Hall*. On a sunny afternoon somewhere on at least one version of what some would call Planet Earth, Arthur felt inspired to ask a pointed question.

"What do you think about the equator, simply saying the first thing that comes to mind?" he asked her.

She responded, "Well, Cubans sometimes visit Ecuador."

He said, "That's a peculiar answer. Do you want to know the first thing I thought about for the equator before asking for your first thought on it?"

She answered slowly and wryly, "Yes, no, maybe, so."

He chuckled. "Well, which will it be?"

She teased, "So, maybe, no, yes."

He chuckled and giggled, then said, "I'll take that to mean that you concluded with a 'yes.'"

After that, they both remained silent for about ten seconds.

She felt confused by his pregnant pause, then asked, "Well, are you going to say out loud what your first thought about it just a little while ago was?"

He grinned, then answered, "If someone mentions the Spring Equinox out loud to another person, then many listeners might assume it to mean the Spring Equinox as from the perspective of the Northern Hemisphere. However, this sort of thing depends. In the regular calendar most popular nowadays, the first Equinox each year is a Spring Equinox, if from a Northern Hemisphere perspective. However, by that same calendar, the second Equinox each year is a Spring Equinox if considered from a Southern Hemisphere perspective. But what about the equator? If a person stands with one foot in the Northern Hemisphere and one foot in the Southern Hemisphere, then how does that person as of that instant on the equator relate to the seasons, the equinoxes, and the solstices? Such an observer would then and there be experiencing all seasons and no seasons."

She responded, "You're making me feel like I'm about to drop dead from taking an equalizer tranquilizer!"

THE END.

Chapter 7: A Penultimate Thought

Sometimes in recent years I have wondered whether Olivia Newton-John (1948-2022) might have been able to survive much deeper into old age if she had done one or more things differently, such as to have had the mysterious level of reality not bring back to her the cancer that she escaped for decades (only to later encounter when it came back around the mountain of the unknown when it revisited her). Regarding a very high percentage of the dead, we the living can occasionally ponder such an imponderable of what-ifs. Although I have hypothesized along many different lines, the one glaring thing that seems to stick out over and over again is the choice of Christopher Pariseleti (c.1971-2013) to commit suicide in 2013 at a then-home of Mr. Easterling and Ms. Newton-John. (Cf. https://www.wpbf.com/article/olivia-newton-john-s-home-site-of-possible-suicide-police-say/1318483 "Olivia Newton-John's home site of possible suicide, police say." WPBF News; WPBF; August 19, 2013; as accessed on January 6, 2025.) We the living might not ever know for sure more than a microscopic percentage of the most mysterious sides. Circa December 1999 I demonstrated hardline skepticism toward all religion and all spirituality in conversation, and Psychiatrist Jennifer ("Jenna") Saul responded to me, "Everyone believes in a little magic." Of course, that generalization is not quite universal, as a person worked up thoroughly into an extremely restrictive interpretation of logic and science, much the way that several notable philosophers and scientists have done over the millennia, that person can go into the realm of an absolute rejection of all types of religion, spirituality, magic, and mysterious causation, other than to lump together all mysteries into (as some ancients in some sense placed into the public domain via statements from over twenty-one centuries ago) either in this or in essentially identical verbiage, "There has to be a nonreligious, nonspiritual, nonmagical, unmysterious explanation to everything, it's just that we don't have the full, scientific wherewithal to fully obtain all those explanations." Those would be among "the nobodies" implicit in Dr. Jennifer Saul's aforementioned late-20th-century statement. In contrast, it does seem evident that a major percentage of living humans do exhibit being among "the everybodies" / "the set of allegedly everybody or allegedly virtually everybody" explicit in Jenna Saul's late-20th-century "everybody believes" statement, as most people accept either the likelihood or the definitude of actual reality of at least a trace of religion, spirituality, magic, and/or mysterious causation, in accordance with how to sum up mysteries into (as some ancients in some sense placed into the public domain via statements from over twenty-one centuries ago) either in this or in essentially identical verbiage, "There has to be at least a little bit of religious, spiritual, magical, and mysterious reality, no matter how much a given mind might believe in the ability to explain each and every mysterious, magical, spiritual, or religious thing away into straightforward sciences."

Let us let go of specific individuals and specific relations for a little while and consider an entire category. Imagine a category in which one person's death winds up causing another person or multiple others to strongly gravitate toward a death spiral, making it extremely difficult for them to avoid dying in the wake. That is, whether with tending to die within ten minutes, within ten years, or whatever. Here is the rub: *If two parties dominate a country's politics and one of them dies, whether by what some would allege to be a suicide, a murder, a justified killing in self-defense, or a hybrid thereof, then the legacy of the death of the one could—either directly or indirectly—prove a difficult challenge to the long-term survival prospects of the other.* This might lead to a daisy chain of party deaths in the long run. *Party 19 and Party 20 fight each other, and Party 19 dies. Party 21 emerges as a powerhouse, and it fights with Party 20, which dies. Party 22 emerges as a powerhouse and fights Party 21. Etc. Etc., &c.*

—M. James Blair, January 6-8, 2025; Houston, Texas, United States of America

CONCLUSION

To: All Political Parties

Cc: Anyone Else Who May Ever Read This

From: Maurice James Blair {The Author of This Book}

Subject: Shape Up or Ship Out

Date: January 5, 2025

For sentient beings to become enlightened—to whatever degree that may involve salvation, conscience, justice, equality, equity, meritocracy, liberty, and anything else of extraordinary worth to beings and their abilities to help others—is essential to their long-term well-being.

However, any specific political party, pair of political parties, trio of political parties, or other combination of political parties is in some sense expendable in the long run in the quest by sentient beings to achieve salvation, conscience, justice, equality, equity, meritocracy, liberty, enlightenment, and/or whatever else would be among the greatest and noblest of possibilities, because political parties that repeatedly fail to honor and respect major swathes of the populations of sentient beings tend to reap what they sow and can veer toward becoming replaced by better political parties. Think about how many political parties have bitten the dust over the millennia. Your party or parties could eventually become next to bite the dust and go extinct.

This is both the clear and coherent opening statement of this book and the clear and coherent closing statement of this book. From entrance to exit. From alpha to omega. From Om to Ah.